C000257081

THE WORKING WOMEN'S GUIDE TO MENOPAUSE

WHEN THE HEAT IS ON, DON'T SWEAT IT!

GAIL GIBSON

RUBY MCGUIRE

Dear Kerry

Be kind to yourself

Gail
x

The Working Women's Guide to Menopause
When the Heat is On. Don't Sweat It!

Copyright © 2021 by Gail Gibson and Ruby McGuire.
All rights reserved.

The book or any portion thereof may not be reproduced or used in any
manner whatsoever without the express written permission of the
publisher except for the use of brief quotations in a book review.

Strenuous attempts have been made to credit all copyrighted materials
used in this book. All such materials and trademarks, which are referenced
in this book, remain the full property of the respective copyright owners.
Every effort has been made to obtain copyright permission for material
quoted in this book. Any omissions will be rectified in future editions.

Cover image by: mrcreativepk
Book design by: Lori Colbeck

ISBN: 978-1-8383538-2-7 (eBook)
ISBN: 978-8-8383538-3-4 (print)

This book is dedicated to all the incredible women across the world, running their own business or working in a corporate role whilst navigating the journey through menopausal change.

Because we know that life does not stop when menopause starts.

There is another way.

It's mindset over menopause.

CONTENTS

INTRODUCTION

Three years and thirty-six 'buzz chat' virtual walks later. We were talking one day whilst trying to book in our next session and failing miserably due to menopausal brain fog. In that moment, Gail jokingly said, 'We should write a book on this and do it fast before we forget what we want to say', and so the idea for this book was born.

You are probably wondering what a buzz chat is. A buzz chat, as coined by us, is a regular call, where we hold each other accountable for mini-goals we are working on, to challenge, inspire, motivate, and uplift us, celebrate our successes, and co-coach each other. Our buzz chats have become a strong support mechanism for us, even more so, as we are on opposite sides of the world, with Ruby in Scotland, and Gail in Malaysia. Our collaborative relationship continues to evolve and is positive, fun, and progressive, although we need to keep reminding each other what we said we would work on. Brain fog!

We are both Accredited Master Coaches with the IAPC&M (The International Authority of Professional Coaching and Mentoring). We have both been working with our respective coaching clients, in small business and corporate, through our own menopause phase and have experienced different degrees of menopausal symptoms in this time.

We recognise that life does not stop just because we women go through menopause. From sleepless nights to sweats and forgets, and cardigans on and off, repeatedly. Our bodies change, our emotions too, but life and business carry on regardless.

As you read the real-life experiences of women in this book, we imagine you will notice and be able to relate to similar and unique challenges you are facing or have faced, whether you are a small business owner or in a corporate role.

This brings us to why we decided to write this book. We wanted to share our experience of menopause and invite other women in business or in the corporate world to share their experiences. Throughout the book, we share a little on the serious side of menopause to give you a taste of the science behind it. On the flipside it is the hilarious menopausal moments, such as Ruby's Chicken story, and Gail's Waterfall story, together with more funny stories shared by the women who feature in the book, that we guarantee will bring a smile to your face.

We coach and mentor in different business areas, Gail with corporate leaders and Ruby with self-employed business owners. While we have approached the book from different perspectives, based on the work we deliver to our clients, we know that the mindset techniques shared are highly effective during the menopausal journey, no matter which area you work in.

Our book aims to help you realise you are not on your own through this journey. We provide practical tips, strategies, and tools (we use daily) to help you, as a working woman, navigate your way through the symptoms and ultimately be kind to yourself through the process.

The co-authors recognise and respect gender diversity. As advocates for gender equality, this book is for anyone who identifies as a woman, transgender, non-binary, and/or other gender-diverse person, who has a menstrual cycle, and is likely to experience menopause.

The book's writing style includes the terms 'woman' and 'women'; however, the co-authors would like to note that these references do not overlook the changes in gender diversity. Being inclusive in approach, the book is practical in nature and accessible to all.

Whatever your position as a professional woman, we hope The Working Women's Guide to Menopause: When the Heat it On, Don't Sweat It! will help you deal with life, and manage your mindset and workload, to thrive through the change and beyond.

MEET THE AUTHORS

**Gail Gibson: Master Performance Coach,
Author, Speaker**

Known as the Can Do coach, award-winning master performance coach, international speaker, podcast host, and author, Gail Gibson, delivers a unique style of 'Can Do' coaching with proven results in enabling her clients to break through the frustration of stagnant or unfulfilled personal and professional growth. The simple, yet incredibly effective coaching techniques she has honed and developed, have led to life-changing transformations in mindset, and personal performance for business and corporate leaders in the UK, US, Australia, and Asia.

A published author (Making Connections: How to Network Effectively to Build Better Business Relationships, 2009; The Rise of SEE-19© Leadership: See Beyond and Become the Leader You Are Born to Be, 2021; The Working Women's Guide to Menopause: When the Heat is On. Don't Sweat It, 2021) and inspirational speaker on mindset, peak personal performance, and SEE-19© Leadership.

Gail hosts an uplifting weekly podcast, The Can Do Way, featuring guests from across the globe who share amazing stories of growth, resilience, and success.

A self-confessed book addict and voracious reader, green tea drinker, and a lover of keeping fit in the great outdoors – her 'green' gym.

Gail lives with her husband in Malaysia.

**Ruby McGuire: Business & Mindset Queen,
Master Coach, Master Mentor, Trainer,
Author, Speaker**

Ruby McGuire, Business & Mindset Queen, helps service-based solopreneurs create a success mindset and step up as Queens (aka CEO's) to grow their business. She loves helping her clients create success by working in 90-day blocks and setting challenges to push through fear.

After eleven years working corporately in HR and consultancy, Ruby has worked freelance running Rock Your Fabulous Biz for many years.

Her expertise means she is a sought-after coach, mentor, trainer, speaker, author. She is an Accredited Master Coach and Accredited Master Mentor trained in NLP, Emotional Freedom Technique (EFT) and Mind Your Mind Techniques. She is also the Head of CPD for the International Authority for Professional Coaching & Mentoring.

A blogger, podcaster, and writer of several books, including Ruby's Coaching Gems (A plethora of 'bling' to grow your coaching biz) Little Book of Visibility Tips, the IAPC&M book How to Win & Keep Clients 2019, The Working

Women's Guide to Menopause: When the Heat is On. Don't Sweat It, 2021, with more on the way. You will always find her surrounded by books with a cappuccino in her hand (She says, "preferably Whittard Vanilla please").

She is an advocate of having fun outside of your life and business and took the brave decision in 2020 to market her business without social media. A mum of a blended family of three girls, she spends her free time making hand-made cards, exploring her home in Scotland, where she has lived since 2018 with her husband Ian and little dog Lulu, and chickens.

2

PERIMENOPAUSE VS MENOPAUSE

Before we share a selection of tried and tested tips, tools, and techniques to help you maximise your mindset during this phase in your life, we thought it would be best to add a little science to the mix.

We often hear the terms perimenopause and menopause being used together. Each one is a stage in the process of change that we women go through. The symptoms can be interchangeable, depending on the phase you're in. Perimenopause often precedes menopause, although not for all women.

What is Perimenopause?

Perimenopause, meaning 'around menopause', is commonly known as the transition phase before menopause. Perimenopause changes can start up to 10 years before menopause, usually during your '30s or '40s. During perimenopause, hormonal changes begin to happen. Many women begin to experience symptoms such as changes in their period cycle, hot flushes/flushes*, night sweats, and mood swings. As perimenopause progresses toward menopause, oestrogen levels will continue to drop. The actual phase of perimenopause can last from a few months to 4 years. Next stop: menopause.

Note: We have used the English term of hot 'flushes', and British English. Saying that, though, we can't promise there won't be errors. We are only human, after all! As you'll read later, we're all about 80% good enough being good enough. (We are also going through brain fog a lot of the time, so please do give us the benefit of the doubt!)

What is Menopause?

Menopause occurs when oestrogen levels are so low that eggs can no longer be produced. Your periods will stop. When you have had no periods for a full twelve months, you will officially be in menopause phase.

What are the symptoms of perimenopause and menopause?

As you go through these phases, you may experience some, all, or none of these symptoms:

Irregular periods	Night sweats
Breast tenderness	Hot flushes
Weight gain	Depression
Headaches	Anxiety
Loss of sex drive	Mood swings
Poor concentration levels	Insomnia
Forgetfulness	Fatigue
Muscle aches	Dry skin

At this point, we feel it is important to note, that peri-menopause and menopause are phases we experience. A phase is a period that does pass. A phase is not for life.

In an interview, Karen, an outdoor coach, shared how she she focused her mindset on going with the flow of the change. Instead of creating resistance and fighting the symptoms of the life phase, she chose to adjust and be mindful of her thoughts, behaviours, and actions. As a result, she experienced minimal disruption and 'sailed through menopause'.

We invite you to spend some time reflecting on these questions:

What can you do to adopt a similar mindset to win through menopause as Karen did?

Will you resist or embrace the changes you experience?

3

GAIL & RUBY'S JOURNEY

Gail's Menopausal Journey

My menopause journey began in my mid-forties.

I noticed changes in my moods, sleep pattern, energy and concentration levels, body temperature, and monthly cycle. Not all the changes I have mentioned happened at once. It was gradual. *The* change had arrived.

At first, I experienced little trouble from perimenopausal symptoms. I accepted my monthly cycle was heading to its destination. The frequency of my cycle became intermittent from one, two or three months to the next. Fortunately, having only suffered painful PMS up to my mid-twenties meant this change in frequency had zero impact on my life.

One significant factor I did experience was the disruption of my sleep pattern. I have been a light sleeper throughout my life, yet have woken up feeling rested and recharged.

However, my sleep became intermittently interrupted by night sweats and bathroom visits. On occasion, after a restless sleep, I would feel groggy and exhausted. This was an unusual feeling, yet one I had to accept and cope with.

As a fit person, who exercises daily, a drop in energy level was noticeable. But, without warning, to suddenly experience bouts of lethargy was foreign to me. From a groggy morning, there have been times when by mid-afternoon, I have needed a nap.

A memorable menopause moment I had; I like to call 'The Waterfall'.

The Waterfall Story

It was summer. While waiting in line at the post office, in a cool air-conditioned space, I suddenly turned into a human waterfall. From the top of my head to my toes, sweat cascaded down my body. I could feel my face getting warmer and warmer. All I wanted to do was take all my clothes off to cool down. I remember feeling soaked, uncomfortable, and unable to do anything to control what was happening. Do I stand in line with a puddle at my feet or go home to dry off? What I thought lasted an eternity was over within minutes. My body temperature returned to normal, and the cooling air was a welcome relief.

Stepping into my shoes as founder and director of a coaching and leadership consultancy, menopause did affect my working life for a short period.

From the personal experiences already mentioned, I felt the change in my energy and concentration levels caused the most impact. In two words – brain fog. This fuzzy mind block could happen anytime, during a conversation with a client in a coaching session, as I wrote an email, or while presenting a talk/webinar. It would strike without warning.

Picture this: I was prepared and ready to ask a question or share information, yet no words came out when I opened my mouth to speak. Who had kidnapped my thoughts and caused this momentary lapse in mental performance? Fortunately, brain fog played a minor role, yet one worthy of winning a best-supporting award for dramatic effect. I believe my brain fog may have been fuelled by disrupted sleep, hormonal fluctuations, and lower energy levels. These three things reduced my ability to think and communicate effectively.

Now in my early fifties, I reflect on how I continue to manage my mindset and the impact of menopausal symptoms in my life.

The night sweats and body temperature fluctuations were over within a couple of months. With these symptoms gone, my sleep shifted into being deeper and more restful. I felt recharged and energised on waking. Hand in hand with an improved sleep pattern, I noticed my brain fog had disappeared. On the odd occasion, I have a mild mental block, which I know is normal for most people.

My menopause management tools:

1. Watch what you eat and how it impacts your behaviour, habits, and thoughts
2. Drink plenty of water to flush your system, to keep you satisfied for longer between meals, and to maintain an agile and alert mindset
3. Prioritise self-care. When you need a break, take time out for yourself, and improve time management and boundaries in your work/life
4. Commit to daily exercise, and get outside in the fresh air, to keep your mind, body, and self at a peak personal performance level
5. Discover your Productive Best work hours and dedicate this time to get priority/urgent/important tasks completed
6. Build powerful and winning habits in your day to better manage your mindset and menopause such as Success Lists, Power Hour, Whitespace, Procrastination & Productivity Hacks
7. Share your journey with others, those in your circle of friends, and with work colleagues. Raise awareness of menopause in the workplace. Encourage and cultivate an inclusive culture of

care and communication and remove the taboo label. The more we talk about menopause, the greater opportunity we allow for awareness and acceptance to normalise menopause in the wider community, that is life.

My one piece of advice to women in business or corporate who are approaching or going through menopause:

Give yourself permission to go with the flow. Why fight this natural process in life? It is your unique experience, your personal journey, whether you have a challenging or easy time. Menopause is a life phase you *can* manage with the right mindset and tools.

Do not sweat it, it is a life phase. It will pass.

Ruby's Menopausal Journey

I think I have had it all happen when it comes to menopause. It started with the hot flushes a few years ago, and then about six months before starting to write this book, I was getting more and more symptoms developing. I was asked to list them by a medical herbalist, and I had about 20 symptoms, including insomnia, hot flushes, forgetfulness, pain in my joints, nausea, dry mouth, dry hair, dry skin, the list went on and on.

The most debilitating of them all was anxiety, followed by the hot flushes and pain in my hands, which had a real impact on my business. I would also get quite forgetful, which wasn't great when I was working with clients.

Then came the tears, for no reason.

One example was when my daughter came up for a visit, and I had not seen her for six months due to the global pandemic. Every time I looked at her, I had burst into tears where I was missing her. She was there. I did not need to miss her! It was completely irrational! Thanks, hormones!

Before considering HRT, I wanted to try the non-medical route, so I am currently working with a medical herbalist. I was symptom-free for a while, and then, like anything related to menopause, the mix needs switching up from time to time as menopause progresses.

I find working on my mindset and giving myself permission to take things slower has been helpful to me. I have ramped up self-care. I had a daily routine that included Qi Gong (Tai Chi is a form of Qi Gong), sometimes some (very) basic yoga, meditation and journalling, which really helped. I decided to do more activity and have rekindled my love for dance, so I do seven dance classes a week, and three active recovery classes for strength and mobility. I also eat healthily, choose not to eat much refined sugar, and limit alcohol (especially red wine - that just makes you feel like you have been set on fire!!)

Work-wise, I get very clear about what I want to achieve, set 3 daily goals, and set a Pomodoro Timer (working in 25-minute blocks) I work with radical focus on ONE thing at a time. The combination of 3 goals, 25-minute blocks, and radically focusing on ONE thing at a time has been a game-changer for me. Once I have hit my three goals, I may set some new goals and keep going if I have the energy, or I simply move them onto a different day if my energy runs out.

I've learned that going with the flow is a much easier way to run my business. I have always told myself that 'you're exactly where you need to be right now', and that takes the pressure off.

My one tip - Listen to your body. It is telling you what is possible for you today. Do not push it, be kind to yourself. Tomorrow is a new day.

"Finish each day and be done with it. You have done what you could. Some blunders and absurdities no doubt crept in; forget them as soon as you can. Tomorrow is a new day. You shall begin it serenely and with too high a spirit to be encumbered with your old nonsense."

RALPH WALDO EMERSON

Cause & Effect

Have you ever come across the phrase 'cause and effect' when it comes to being in control of your life? It is a Neuro-Linguistic Programming (NLP)* language pattern and could be costing you lots of time, energy and maybe even dreamie clients. (Dreamie is the name I call ideal clients).

* *A coaching modality that's like having an instruction manual for your mind.*

What is it all about?

If you are at 'EFFECT', someone/something else is in control of your life:

1. One thing causes another (the effect)
2. You blame others for failing
3. You come from a disempowered place because you believe you rely on situations/circum-stances/people to effect change.

If you are at 'CAUSE' you are in control of your life:

1. You create your life
2. You take responsibility for your life and what happens in it
3. You come from a powerful place because you believe you can effect change.

When it comes to menopause, we can find ourselves hating and shaming our bodies when they do not behave the way we want them to. This is when you are at EFFECT.

Being at CAUSE is a much better place to be. From here, you get to create your world, where you are in control and taking responsibility for your life and what happens in it. It is not wishful thinking. It does not mean things will not go wrong. They probably will, that's life, but it is your reaction to them that counts.

It is easier to blame things outside of ourselves, though isn't it? We can pass on all responsibility to someone or something else, it is easier.

Blame does not serve anybody; it will only help you wallow and not act. You can choose to take responsibility for your life. Do not give your power away.

Yes, you might have your challenges with menopause. I know I have many daily challenges to deal with, but I will not let them define me.

DECIDE today that you will not allow your menopausal challenges to define you either. It is only one aspect of your life. Take ownership of your body. Learn what you can about menopause and do what you can to feel your best.

If you are suffering from perimenopause or menopause, know that **you are not on your own:**

We have held interviews with different women throughout the book, where we asked four specific questions. We hope these interviews will help you get some insights on how best to navigate your way through your menopausal journey:

- How did/does menopause affect you in your working life?
- What worked for you to manage and cope with your challenges?
- What advice do you have for professional women who are going through menopause?
- What one piece of advice would you give to other women going through menopause?

You might like to stop reading for a moment and answer them yourself right now.

We have sprinkled anecdotes throughout the book, and at the end of the book, you will be able to meet them properly, where we share their whole story.

When you are going through perimenopause, your emotions can be all over the place. I would say that overall, my feelings have been pretty stable over the years. However, enter my new friend, Perry (perimenopause), and there are some days when my emotions can take over.

The Salmon Story!

Let me tell you about my salmon experience.

I'd been watching a TEDTalk by a neuroscientist who was talking about menopause. As part of her talk, she shared Mediterranean foods that can be helpful to alleviate symptoms. I already eat a healthy diet because I have a lot of food intolerances, so we tend to cook pretty much everything from scratch. She mentioned salmon, which I do not eat very often, so I told my husband and said that maybe we would pick some up next time we go shopping.

Fast forward a few days later, by which time I have completely forgotten about salmon - which was possibly yet another side-effect of my menopause, who knows?! Anyway, I received a phone call from my hubby, who was telling me that he was currently in the supermarket doing the grocery shopping. He told me that he had picked up everything on the list and that he had also picked up some salmon for me.

The rational, non-perimenopausal, Ruby, would have said something along the lines of, 'Ah, thank you, darling, that's really sweet of you to remember.'

However, not this version of Ruby. I burst into tears and felt overwhelming emotion that my lovely husband had remembered a conversation about the salmon.

Through tears streaming down my face, I said to him, "Ah, I can't believe you remembered. That's so kind of you." I felt overcome by his kindness.

"Seriously, what is with the emotions, Universe? You're making me seem like I'm crazy!" I do not even cry that much.

I felt ridiculous, but it was out of my control. The poor guy must have wondered what on earth was going on! We still laugh to this day about the salmon story.

4

FACTS ABOUT MENOPAUSE

Did You Know:

1. In 350BC, Aristotle noticed menopause. The philosopher decided it started at age 40 and noted women could not bear children after age 50
2. In England in the 1800's doctors prescribed a pre-meal mixture of carbonated soda to their menopausal patients and opium and cannabis to curb menopause symptoms
3. In 1821, a French physician named Charles Pierre Louis De Gardanne coined the term la ménépausie (menopause)
4. In 1890, Merck began marketing Ovariin, the first menopause drug made of desiccated and pulverised cow ovaries, as a remedy for menopause symptoms.
5. In 1938, synthetic oestrogen was developed
6. In 1942, Ayerst Laboratories started selling

Premarin, a still-popular oestrogen replacement therapy that helps with menopause symptoms

7. The International Menopause Society was born in 1978 in Jerusalem during the 2nd International Congress on Menopause

8. In 2001, "Menopause: The Musical" premiered, featuring 25 comedic songs about menopause, covering topics such as food cravings, hot flushes, and memory loss

9. In 2014, World Menopause Month was created by the World Health Organisation (WHO) and the International Menopause Society (IMS) The aim of the month is to raise awareness of the stage in a woman's life when she stops menstruating and to help women understand the possible health issues associated when approaching, during, and after menopause

10. World Menopause Day is celebrated on October 18 each year

11. Menopause means the ceasing of menstruation and is taken from the Greek words *pausis* (pause) and *mēn* (month)

12. Symptoms of menopause differs globally - in the West, hot flush, in Japan, shoulder pain and in India, low vision are the hallmarks of menopause

13. Menopause is considered a *"second spring"* in Chinese culture. It is seen as a positive time of creativity and new beginnings when women often find a new and more confident voice

14. The Japanese term *konenki* translates to

menopause effects. Japanese women experience lower rates of hot flushes and night sweats. Menopause in Japan is viewed as a symptom of the inevitable ageing process, rather than a "revolutionary transition", or a "deficiency disease" in need of management

15. Based in the UK, the International Menopause Society (IMS) brings together the world's leading experts to collaboratively study and share knowledge about all aspects of ageing in women.

5

MORNING ROUTINES

Gail's Morning Routine

It's a State of Mindset

Peak personal performance is a key driver in my life.

As a leadership and performance coach, I help business, and corporate leaders achieve peak personal performance.

As an individual, I have always been an active person.

I was actively encouraged to play sports from my childhood, including netball, tennis, basketball, squash, swimming, cycling, hiking, running, and ballet.

Through life experience, I have learnt to embed the positive habit of physical exercise, which helps me continue to achieve my peak personal performance. Fast forward to today; at age 52, I speed walk daily, play tennis weekly, cycle, swim and run.

Peak personal performance is not only about movement and exercise.

I live and breathe a holistic approach to personal performance by focusing on mind, body, and soul. It is vital to take care of your physical, mental, cognitive, and emotional health.

Self-care is a positive routine I choose to focus on and commit to.

Self-care has become my priority go-to habit of winning through the challenges of menopause. When I make time to look after myself, I feel relaxed in mind, body, and soul. In this state of being, I am calm, focused, and grateful, which help me better manage the changing dynamics of menopause.

Life does not stop just because we women go through menopause.

By continuing my whole body, daily fitness habit, I have found that many difficult symptoms of perimenopause and menopause have been reduced. For me, the increased body movement teamed with my Can Do mindset serves to 'sweat out' any symptoms. In addition, because I love to exercise, this habit has now eliminated all hot flushes and night sweats (even in a hot and humid tropical climate), allowing my sleep to be deep and restful.

Ask yourself: What positive habit or routine will I continue doing as I go through menopause to reduce/eliminate my challenging symptoms?

Or, if you have yet to discover what works for you, ask, what habit or routine will I commit to building to reduce/eliminate my challenging symptoms?

To help you plan, let me share why I love my morning routine and what I do.

There are plenty of positive reasons why I love my morning routine. I can focus on my inner and outer self during this time to awaken my mind, body, and soul. Each morning, for my outer/physical self to activate and ignite myself into action, I power up and switch on with energetic outdoor activity. For my inner self, I embrace the start of a new day in my life. I spend quiet 'me time, being reflective, grateful and mindful.

Here is my daily 2-hour morning routine:

1. **Stretch**. Upon waking, I stretch like a cat before getting out of bed. I reach my fingertips to the top of the bed head and point my toes to the end of the mattress. I alternate sides to get a good stretch

2. **Flex**. I flex my feet and toes to lengthen and warm up my muscles

3. **Hydrate**. I drink 1 litre of room temperature water

4. **Move**. Fitness kit and shoes on, and out the door, I go. My daily goal is 10K steps. I fast walk or run or swap between the two, 5K steps on a dawn

walk, and 5K steps (with my husband) on a
sunset walk

5. **Hydrate.** Post walk/run, I drink 1 litre of room
temperature water

6. **Post Exercise**. I do 30 pushups and then hold
in a dog pose. Next, I sit in the ancient squat
position (feet flat on the floor, knees hip-width
apart, buttocks almost touching ankles). The pose
takes time to master. It is brilliant as an extra
special hamstring and lower back stretch. Say
goodbye to any lower back pain, often associated
with sitting for long periods. Try it during your
working day

7. **Grateful**. I say aloud three things I am grateful
for – the gift of today, my most precious gifts
(husband, parents, family, friends, clients,
colleagues, health, wealth, business), and my
learning from yesterday and my intention for
today

8. **Meditation**. I sit in silence for 20 minutes and
focus on my breath, allowing my thoughts to come
and go, and filter

9. **Nutrition**. I eat a healthy breakfast of two boiled
eggs and a homemade Power Juice (mango,
turmeric, orange, lemon, fresh ginger, and apple
cider vinegar)

10. **Tea**. I spend 30 minutes reading a book or
listening to a short podcast while sipping fresh
green tea.

You may be thinking, how do you set aside 2-hours a day to 'power up' your mind, body, and soul?

It is important to remember, the secret to your success comes from finding and building a habit or routine that works for YOU. So whether you run a small business from home, or you are a corporate executive, it is your choice to create a self-care routine or 'Me time' to activate, and ignite your mind, body, and soul into action. For you, this may be a 15-minute walk outside on your lunch break, 30 minutes reading a book or listening to a podcast while you eat and hydrate, and 15 minutes in quiet 'whitespace' reflection.

Ask women you know who have experienced menopause for their tips and tricks to prioritise self-care.

Choose one or two to try. If it works,
carry on. If not, choose another way that works best for you. When you listen to and take notice of what is happening to your mind, body, and soul as you go through menopause, I have no doubt you will tune in the right habit or routine that really helps reduce or eliminate your most challenging symptoms.

We would love to hear about the tried and tested ways our readers have embraced self-care as a positive and progressive routine in their menopause journey. Feel free to share your stories of success with us. See the What's

Next section at the back of this book for contact info.

Ruby's Morning Routine

Having a morning routine is important, no matter what age you are in life. To be able to help other people you first need to look after yourself. When you are going through perimenopause/menopause, it is even more crucial for you to make the time for self-care.

I find that having a morning routine sets me up nicely for the day. I choose to wake up a bit earlier each day to have time to look after myself before my busy day begins. My list of things that I like to do when I get up is quite long. However, I simply adjust the timings depending on what time I have available to me each day.

My plans for the day determine the amount of time I give to each area. Sometimes, if I am feeling indulgent, I can spend an hour doing my morning routine. Other times, I might fit it into 10 to 15 minutes.

Here is a list of the things that I do every morning to take care of myself:

1. Drink a Glass of Water

When I remember to hydrate the minute I get up, I then remember to drink water throughout the day. Drinking water is vital under normal circumstances, but even more critical when you keep having hot flushes every few minutes (or Tropical Moments, as one lady I used to work with called it!)

2. Headspace

I like to do a few minutes of meditation each day. Truthfully, I am no angel. I have never really got past 10 minutes a day scenario. What is key for me is that I am doing it consistently. I really notice the days that I do not do meditation. Sometimes, I might only manage as much as 3 minutes of meditation using my Headspace app. However, those 3 minutes make a big difference to how my day goes.

3. Morning Pages

Morning Pages is a concept by Julia Cameron, who wrote a book called The Artists Way. She recommends you write three sides of an A4 sheet of paper every day, with what she calls a stream of consciousness. Essentially, you are downloading everything that is in your head onto sheets of paper. When you first begin to write, you might find yourself thinking about all the things that your day will entail. From doing the washing, clearing the garden, cooking dinner, to conversations that you might need to have, to work that needs to get done, etcetera, etcetera. It is a great way to start clearing your mind and to get some clarity.

I tend to ask myself this question each day:

What do I need to know/do today?

Initially, you will have all the mental chatter going through your mind, and as that clears, new ideas, inspiration, and guidance pop into your head. I find morning pages so valuable that if I could only do one thing as my morning routine this would be it.

I find when I do not do my Morning Pages, I am pretty scattered. I find it hard to concentrate and focus. I also find by doing Morning Pages that I can make decisions much quicker, again freeing up mental headspace.

4. Gratitude

Every day, before I get out of bed, I think of three things I am grateful for. Over the years, as a family, we also played the gratitude game. This is the same principle, but you think of three things you are grateful for, and you say why. You are not allowed to do any repeats. This is because it allows you to search for amazing new things to be grateful for.

5. Qi Gong/Tai Chi/Yoga

Finally, my morning routine includes doing some form of movement. I am still not entirely over the moon about yoga. I find it quite challenging. I do have a couple of routines that I do like to use though. My go-to movement tends to be either Qi Gong or Tai Chi. I have a couple of little apps that I use, with simple and short sequences that I can squeeze in every day. I usually do 5 to 10 minutes of Qi Gong or Tai Chi a day.

When I have more time and let us be honest, the inclination, I work on learning new sequences that are longer. This tends to be more random though.

It is All About You!

In reality, what I do for my morning routine is irrelevant. The important thing is for you to think about what YOU need for your self-care.

The BIG thing that you need to know is that self-care is not just a tick box exercise. There are four key areas to self-care:

- **Physical** - healthy and regular eating, exercise, rest, relaxation, sleep
- **Mental** - unplugging from technology, doing something non-work related, learning something new, setting boundaries, problem-solving
- **Emotional** - relationships, friendships, community, talking through problems, forgiveness
- **Spiritual** - connecting with nature, meditation, quiet time, mindfulness, your spiritual practice.

Let us start with a Self-Care Quiz to determine how well you are taking care of yourself already. This quiz is just for fun, it is not scientific in any way, but it will give you an idea of where you can take care of yourself even better.

Self-Care Quiz

How good are you at taking care of yourself? Try out this little quiz to find out.

Score 0 for Never, 1 for Sometimes, 2 for Often, 3 for Always

- I look after my health, ensuring I eat healthily every day, exercise regularly
- I bring relaxation into my routine each day
- I limit my alcohol intake (if you limit your alcohol but you are a smoker, then score 0)
- I get sufficient sleep every single night and listen to what my body needs
- I'm comfortable setting boundaries and saying no to things that aren't right for me
- I allow myself time out from work/family commitments to do something nice
- I have a list of things to do/places to go that lift my spirits and help me feel replenished
- I have a fabulous circle of family/friends that support me when I need it
- I take time to go offline – switching off all technology for a set period
- I always feel calm and ready for whatever I face in the day ahead
- I have some good daily routines
- I take regular short breaks throughout the day to recharge myself.

How did you do? What did you learn about yourself? Did some of them make you smile because you recognised areas for improvement?!

Scores

0-15 What needs to change? Choose one specific area that you can improve that will have the quickest impact.

16-21 – You are doing well, but there is room for improvement. Think about which one of these you need the most, work on that one first and then move on to the next.

22-29 - You understand how valuable self-care is and already reap the benefits of its rewards, but you can still raise those numbers if you put some work in. Keep reminding yourself why this is important.

30-36 - Wow, you are amazing! You have this self-care thing all figured out. Keep it up now.

Here is a list for each self-care area to get you thinking about how you can improve your score.

Physical Self-Care

- Healthy & regular eating – choosing the best foods
- Needs to become part of your overall health strategy
- Missing meals is not healthy
- Make your health a priority
- Water intake
- Exercise
- Move it! Dance, jump, swim, do yoga – just move!
- Stretch
- General Health and Wellbeing

- Medical health check-ups
- Reduce stress (Check out the Linden Method)
- Manage your time
- Rest & relaxation
- Taking breaks from work/during the day
- Learning to switch off
- Me time – massages, aromatherapy, reading, long baths
- Do nothing! Stop doing, start being!
- Sleep
- Bedtime routines
- Switching off time.

'A well-spent day brings happy sleep'.

LEONARDO DA VINCI

Mental Self-Care

- Unplugging from technology - do you?
- Doing something non-work related - This includes not working 'in your head'!
- Learning something new, a new skill
- Building your knowledge
- Setting boundaries - this will be a whole chapter, so look out for it
- Respecting your time and yourself
- Structure/Planning

- Creating a plan for your day/week/month, mini-goals
- Problem solving
- Keeping your mind alive!
- Fulfilling work
- Goal setting
- Include a daily check-in – what is working/not, review
- Finding purpose and meaning
- Living in alignment with your values
- Decluttering.

Emotional Self-Care

- Relationships
- Connection – hugs, kisses ... ahem ;)
- Beware of your roles – are you over-helping people? Taking on too much responsibility?
- Friendships
- Strong support network – coffee with friends/days out
- Community
- Hobbies / social interaction
- Contribution – to family, friends, your world
- Mindset
- Talking through things - not bottling things up
- Positive self-talk & beliefs – affirmations
- Self-love & self-compassion
- Give yourself permission to be happy, change your mind, experience your emotions.

- Say yes to what you really want, not what you think you should
- Positive memories
- Forgiveness
- Freeing yourself of things that are holding you back.

Spiritual Self-Care

- Connecting with nature
- Country walks, seaside, fresh flowers
- Being still - pause. Remember, you are a human 'being', not a human 'doing'
- Meditation, breathing exercises
- Sing, read, dance, laugh, play, cook, be artistic.
- Self-reflection
- journalling, poetry, creativity, let go of what did not work
- Community
- Volunteering
- Talking through problems
- Not bottling things up
- Forgiveness for self and others
- Letting go of your worries, problems, and anger (more on that soon)
- Gratitude
- Enjoy simple everyday pleasures – count them!
- Practice being grateful – choose the #1 thing you are grateful for right now.

'Self-care is not about self-indulgence, it's about self-preservation'.

AUDRE LORDE

What if you cannot stop working, and you find it difficult?

I know you might tell yourself that it is not that easy to stop working.

Stopping can be tricky.

I get it, I am a workaholic. Even when I am not working, I am working in my head.

Here are a few simple strategies that will help you ease off work:

- Set clear boundaries, i.e. I will stop work at 5.00pm, or I will leave the office by 5.30pm
- Work out where your time goes. You might find you can streamline tasks and work fewer hours
- Drop the perfectionism - 80% good enough is, well, good enough
- MAKE time for you and MAKE time to play.

'Self-compassion is simply giving the same kindness to ourselves that we would give to others'.

CHRISTOPHER GERMER

Here are a few thought-provoking questions for you to dive into:

What impact is not looking after your health having/going to have?

What needs to happen for you to put your health and well-being first?

'When we keep borrowing against our future by poorly protecting our energy, there is a predictable outcome of either slowly running out of gas or prematurely crashing and burning'.

THE ONE THING BY GARY KELLER

Love your body. What do you think when you hear/read that?

What do you need to do today to feed your body/mind with the good stuff?

> *'Feed your body with good food, feed your mind with good thoughts'.*
>
> TONY ROBBINS

What are you going to do differently because of reading this?

What support/resources would help you?

How will you ensure that your health and wellbeing now become a priority?

Mini Self-Care Plan

It's time to create a mini Self-Care Plan. Here is a quick reminder of the four key areas and a few examples under each area for you to consider:

- **Physical** – Healthy & regular eating, exercise, general health and wellbeing, rest, relaxation, sleep
- **Mental** – Unplugging, learning new skills, boundaries, problem-solving, fulfilling work, goal setting, finding purpose and meaning
- **Emotional** – Relationships, friendships, community, mindset, forgiveness
- **Spiritual** – Connecting with nature,

mindfulness, singing, creativity, self-reflection, gratitude.

Which of the above areas do you think you need to work on?

(Choose one and commit to working on it as an area of self-care this month)

For this coming month, I choose to work on …

Often one of the things that happens when we neglect our self-care is we stop doing some of those things that we really enjoy. It might be singing, dancing, cooking, yoga, rock climbing, swimming, reading, going to the pictures, bubble baths, hairdressers, pampering, online classes, crafting etc.

What things do you love doing?

(Choose one thing you love and aim to fit it into your schedule this week)

For this coming week, I choose to add this fabulous thing into my schedule …

If you'd prefer not to write in your book, like us, you can download our lovely Reflective Workbook that contains all of the questions we've asked you in one place. Find out more in Chapter 12, Reflective Workbook.

6

MANAGING YOU

Protect Your Time

Another area that you might need to work on around self-care is protecting your time. If you are running a business or in the corporate world, you are likely already a very busy woman and protecting your time will be something you have to do. When you are in perimenopause or menopause, this becomes even more important as your energy levels may drop.

'When you say yes to others, you are saying no to yourself'.

PAULO COELHO

When you are going through menopause, you are dealing with all day-to-day life scenarios. You then have to manage your wellbeing on top of that. So while it is admirable to help and support people, you should do it because you want to, not because you feel you 'should' or 'have' to. You should also be mindful of your energy levels, and how you feel in general.

The Wisdom of Getting Older

As you get older, you get wiser. You might have spent most of your life so far focused on other people, which can be part of the problem of going through this life change. The fantastic thing is that you get to choose how you live your life going forward.

Are You Ready To Change?

When you do, you will:

- Gain control
- Get your power back
- Be nicer to know!
- Get time to do the things you love
- Feel more confident.

What can you do about it?

- Set boundaries and practice saying 'no'
- Remember the 'I' word
- Practice self-care.

Setting Boundaries

Boundaries are incredibly powerful. They are a way for you to preserve energy, maintain self-respect and honour your time. They are an absolute necessity when you are navigating your way through life.

I started on my path of boundary setting a few years ago, and oh, what a journey it has been! As you will find out, your boundaries will be constantly pushed, you will make mistakes and forget about them, only to have to reset them again, but hang in there. They are amazing and have the potential to change your life.

The problem is, we care. We like to help people and go over and above to ensure people have what they need. I can remember managing a residential home for the elderly years ago and being told to let people have responsibility for their own lives too, as you are empowering them. We think we must do it all for everyone, but they do not learn that way, and worse it can be damaging, as they no longer believe they can do things on their own.

The wonderful world of boundary setting takes you down a path. It can be uncomfortable, as you have to re-train people how you want to be treated, but it is super important. On the other hand, by taking on too much, you can end up pushing yourself into overwhelm.

Here are some examples of where you might be having your boundaries pushed but not have even noticed:

- People are overstepping the mark in your working arena, whether that is your own business/corporate
- You are answering work emails late at night and/or helping more than is required of you
- You are not switching off and having downtime. You say to yourself, 'Just one more little job and then I am done'. Maybe that's just me!
- People keep asking you to do things for them, despite you feeling as though you could not take on another single thing
- You are getting a bit irritated, or maybe annoyed when asked to do something else because you feel taken advantage of, or you are panicking about what you already must do, and one more thing might push you over the edge.

If you want to stop overwhelm, then it is worth working on boundaries.

Boundary setting is like drawing an imaginary line around you and deciding what is and is not right for you.

It is essential to set boundaries in our lives. Without boundaries, people will take advantage, and we are left feeling as though our opinions/feelings do not matter, hence the saying, 'Give them an inch, and they'll take a mile'. The thing is, if you have always been someone that does everything everyone else wants to do and you do not say what you want, then setting boundaries is the antidote.

Believe it or not, people use you the way you trained them to. So, to have a better or different relationship, you need to re-train them. You have to 'train' the people around you to know that things will be different around here now and that you want some of your own needs met, which can cause some issues. Conflict may arise. Sadly, some people might not like the new you! You may have arguments, lose friends/potential clients, maybe even clients, and have relapses. People need to re-learn how to be around you.

How do you know when to set a boundary?

- If someone is asserting their rights over yours
- Time stealers
- When people are always getting their own way
- When you feel like a doormat
- One-way toxic relationships.

You may have recognised some scenarios where you need to set boundaries. The examples above are just a few of them that you may have already come across.

Drawing a Line

 Here is a simple exercise for figuring out what you do/do not want to continue in your life.

Get out two pieces of paper.

Think about all the things that you currently do and how well they are working for you. On one piece of paper:

- Write down your needs
- Write down how you spend your time
- Notice where you are people-pleasing.

On the second sheet of paper, draw a big circle in the middle of the page and write 'Me' in the middle.

Let us say you are answering emails at night, and it makes you feel irritated, write 'Answering Emails' OUTSIDE of your circle.

It might be that you have a few minutes each day focusing on yourself, then you might write down 'Me Time' INSIDE your circle.

Once you have brainstormed all of the ideas, start to think about how things would be different in your life if you were just dealing with those things INSIDE of your circle.

Now comes the tough bit. What boundaries can you put in place for those things on the OUTSIDE of your circle?

So, for the answering emails scenario, it might be that you decide one of the following:

You will have a cut off time at night, after which you will not answer emails.

You will not reply to your client for a couple of days and let them figure out a strategy themselves. Often, they will. I know I do that sometimes; I will ask a friend for help, and then because they are busy and I do not hear from them, I will figure it out myself anyway. I then wonder why I asked, but it is just about reassurance that you are on the right track. Same with your clients.

Instead of answering their query, you tell them that it would be better explored in a coaching/consultation session/appointment/meeting etc. and book one in.

You MUST learn how to say 'No' or you will burn yourself out!

The next time you say 'yes' to someone else, ask yourself why you are saying 'no' to yourself*.

(*adapted from Paulo Coelho quote).

It is not selfish – it is self-care.

Being a people pleaser can impact both your personal and business life. It can make you feel frustrated, anxious, overwhelmed. It is bad for your health and is draining and exhausting!

When setting boundaries, be kind to yourself – allow it to take the time that it needs. You WILL have setbacks. You WILL revert back to old ways at times. Keep working on it. The rewards are SO worth the effort.

It is not just about making commitments to yourself to set boundaries and do better, though. What about when someone says something to you that you do not like? Your silence is, in effect, approving what they said, so what should you do differently?

Get Some Clarity Around Your Boundaries

Spend a few minutes journalling around the following questions:

- Who or what do I need to say 'no' to?
- What is the benefit of holding onto this 'you are more important than I am' ethos?
- What needs to happen for me to honour and value myself?
- What is the worst that could happen if I speak up for what I want or believe is right?
- What would be a great way to overcome that?
- What conversation do I need to have to explain how I feel and the way I want my needs met?
- How do I vent my feelings?
- Who do I have in my life that can act as a confidante to express my feelings to?
- Where in life would I like to be more assertive?
- When I say 'yes' to others, how am I saying 'no' to myself?
- What difference would that make to me?

Practice Flexing Your 'NO' Muscles

Say 'No'... Easy? No - but practice makes perfect.

We are worried about what people might think or say if we ask for what we need. This is because we have been taught to be polite and nice.

Start to say the word 'no' in lots of different areas of your life:

- Say 'no' to people you do not know
- Say 'no' to people who cross your boundaries
- Say 'no' to things you don't want to do
- Say 'no' to friends/family/colleagues/negativity
- Say 'no' to people who expect too much.

Practice Saying 'No'

(Here are some examples of how you might say 'no')

- "I would love to, but I am already committed to ..."
- "That sounds lovely, but I have committed to myself some precious 'me' time while the house is quiet. Another time?"
- "It is really kind of you to think of me. I like to give things my 100% Right now, my priority is 'x' so I would not have the time to dedicate to it and give it the full attention it deserves".
- Offer an alternative ... "I cannot do (date), but I could do (date) if that works for you?"
- "It is a busy month. Let me check my diary when I am back at home, and I will send you over some possible dates".

- "It is not something that feels right for me, but I could put you in touch with ...".

Set a mini-goal, where you aim to get 20 rejections over the next month. The more rejections you get, the easier you will find it to say no yourself. You will build resilience you did not have before.

'There is no rejection, there is only redirection'.

ADAM GRANT

Remember the 'I' word. How often do you use it?

- If it is all about what others want and need, then you are putting others before yourself
- Notice when you're using the words 'others', 'should', 'they', 'he/she', 'sorry.'

Ask these questions:

- "What do I need right now?"
- "What is right for me in this?"
- 'If I park what other people want for a moment, what is it that I truly want?'

Practice Self-Care

- You need to look after yourself – YOU MATTER
- What do you really enjoy? What makes you feel super happy?
- What three daily habits could you create to look after yourself?
- 10-minute read with a cup of tea/coffee
- Leisurely bath etc.

Make space in your diary for you. Book out things you enjoy first, make you a priority.

Journalling

A very powerful tool when working on changing your behaviours around people-pleasing. It can be used to:

- List your accomplishments with regards to boundary setting
- Ask yourself why you chose to say 'yes' or 'no' to a specific thing and what difference it made
- List ways in which you have been authentic in that day, true to yourself and who you are
- Journal your true feelings, using the journal as a way of expressing yourself than bottling things up
- List ways in which you have been more assertive, at work and/or in your personal life
- Note down things that make you happy and do them!

Watch-outs

- Setting boundaries takes time
- Retraining is involved
- They may challenge you/talk about you/fall out with you
- But you are just as important – keep reminding yourself that this is not a bad thing – it is the right thing.

Over to you

- Write down your needs
- Write down how you spend your time
- Notice where you are people-pleasing.

Action

Be kind to yourself – allow it to take the time that it needs.

You WILL have setbacks, you WILL revert, just keep working on it.

The rewards are SO worth the effort.

'Be who you are and say what you feel because those who mind do not matter and those who matter do not mind'.

DR SEUSS

Know When You Do Your Best Work

I think the key to managing your time is knowing when you do your best work.

Are you an early bird or a night owl?

As we know, energy levels can shift massively from one day to the next, even in the day.

You must go with that energy, work with it if you like. While you might want to create world domination, sometimes your body will have different ideas. Some days it can all just feel too much, and you want to throw yourself on the sofa and do nothing.

That is fine, but if this continues for days it will have an impact on your business/career.

Start noticing your energy levels throughout the day.

When you feel like you are dragging yourself around because you are so tired, ask yourself this question:

What one thing is essential right now? (*Choose something that you can do in line with your current energy levels*)

It might be stopping and having a cup of tea.

It might be setting yourself a time within which to work, so instead of a daunting seven-hour day ahead of you, you are just thinking about the next time block.

K.I.S.S

I love to use the acronym KISS. You may know it as Keep It Simple Stupid. However, I am not sure why anyone would want to call themselves stupid, so I call it Keep It Simple Sweetie.

'Simplicity boils down to 2 steps: Identify the essential. Eliminate the rest'.

LEO BABAUTA

If you'd prefer not to write in your book, like us, you can download our lovely Reflective Workbook that contains all of the questions we've asked you in one place. Find out more in Chapter 12, Reflective Workbook.

7

MANAGE YOUR MINDSET

Imperfectly Perfect

Before we dig into mindset I want to talk about perfection. If you are striving for perfection, you will be fighting a losing battle.

When you go through menopause, you can often feel like you are a completely different person. Your face and body are changing internally and externally, the way you react to things is changing, your thought patterns might not be as clear, and you may be experiencing many physical symptoms.

As one of our interviewees, Fiona, said, more people are now treating menopause in the same vein as mental health illness, in that you can take time out to nurture yourself, a duvet day if you like.

While we know we need to work through menopause and understand, we cannot all stop working for ten years and do nothing. We also lay many expectations on our doorstep. We are trying to keep up the same way we have always done, yet often with depleted energy levels and limited resources. We are trying to be Mary Poppins, despite how we are feeling.

'Practically perfect in every way'.

MARY POPPINS

But the thing is, you do not need to be Mary Poppins, or practically perfect, and you probably do not even have the time! Go with 80% perfect, and that needs to be good enough.

In what way are you a perfectionist? Perfectionism is all about having super high standards. The dictionary definition when I Googled it says this – "Refusal to accept any standard short of perfection." Wow, so much pressure! If this is you, then it is time to change. Life gets SO much more fun when you loosen up a bit (I know this from personal experience!).

You might have had this trait throughout your life, or you might find it starting to kick in now. Either way, let's check in to find out what's going on.

Fear of judgement – Ironic really when the most significant person that is judging you is you! You need to help your employees/clients understand that you are going through something right now. You may need to educate them.

Fear of failure – you WILL make mistakes, fact! Make them, learn from them. It is feedback, not failure. You will make mistakes whether you are going through menopause or not. By being kinder to yourself, you're less likely to make as many mistakes as possible.

Fear of 'it' not being good enough – Check the impact, 'How much will this really matter in three months, six months, one year?' We can tend to go micro with our thinking, where we analyse what is happening or has happened. When you go macro instead, you start to see the bigger picture, and you understand that while this is frustrating, it really is not that big a deal in the scheme of things.

Imposter Syndrome – Where you think you're going to be found out. Therefore, it is essential to talk about menopause. It will help the people you work with, or do business with, understand what is going on for you. You are perfectly imperfect.

If you had a friend going through this, what would you say to them? Would you tell them to berate themselves, or would you encourage them to be kind and loving with their body changing on every level?

Perfectionism is problematic at the best of times but even more so when working against yourself when you are going through something that's often out of your control.

Don't let perfectionism ruin your life and/or work. Instead, take some steps to deal with it. Become a work in progress like me!

Perfectionism is self-sabotaging behaviour and does not serve you. It stops you from sharing your unique gifts with the world. It is time to let it go and be imperfectly perfect.

This week I invite you to take some imperfect action. It can be anything. Get that task 80% done and call it finished.

Keeping it Real

If you live in the UK around menopausal age, you may remember the comedian in the late '70s, early '80s, called Les Dawson. He would do a sketch where two women talked to each other about female issues, and they would mouth quietly when they spoke about it. They would not voice any of it out loud properly. This was how it was. Women did not talk about how they were feeling. Thankfully, this has changed.

We are now more likely to speak about what is going on with our bodies. However, there are still times when we feel like we must deal with this on our own. We think that perhaps we are the only one going through this.

When I work with my clients, a massive part of the work I do is around mindset. One of the first things I encourage with clients is to keep it real. I tell them it is important to voice their feelings. Once you voice how you feel, you feel more empowered, and you can deal with your feelings.

Here is a short exercise I share with my business clients around clearing fear or any other unwanted emotion.

Reframe Your Fear Into Fabulousness

What story are you creating about yourself right now? Get it all out on the page. It might be:

- Menopause must be hard
- My mother had bad menopause, which means I must have one too
- I'm finding this all challenging
- Having menopause and trying to work is awkward
- People are judging me
- People will write me off because I am not as good as I used to be
- I'll never be able to pull this off with how I feel
- I'm taking two steps forward and one step back.

Let it all out, baby – it is liberating! Write down any fears in the space below that come up for you as you think about your business. These are all becoming your story, and we want to create a much more fabulous story instead! Be as negative as you want to be. We will be moving on to clearing it all next.

Now, let us do some releasing of all that icky stuff!

I created the acronym for F.E.A.R over brekkie one morning with my lovely hubby and daughter! I was trying to come up with something that helped me to remember the best way to release all this rubbish, and while 'Fear Dump' was an excellent method (where you 'dump' all your fears out on paper), the name did not work for me, for obvious reasons!) So, we got creative, and this is what we got.

You may know the acronym as False Evidence Appearing Real, and yes, that is one way, but let us use my acronym to help release this stuff.

Here is what it stands for (the quick version)

F – **Feelings** - get into the feelings that are coming up for you and write them down

E – **Express** - read them out loud

A – **Acknowledge** - that it is okay to have those feelings, thank them and choose to view things differently from now on

R – **Release** - Choose to release them one by one focusing on each one and saying "I choose to release you now" as you cross each one off the list.

Let it all go and start creating a new, more empowering story.

Here is the longer version:

F = FEELINGS

So, I want you to take one single statement at a time, and then for each of the statements you made above, I want you to get into the actual **feelings** of what might be underneath the statement.

E = EXPRESS

Now it is time to **express** those feelings. It is one thing writing them on paper, but I invite you to give them a bit more power for a moment by reading them out loud. Remember to say one single statement at a time, not all in one go. It is important that we do the releasing of each one, not in a job lot!

A = ACKNOWLEDGE

Feelings come up for a reason. They are our guiding system. We can be all Pollyanna about it and say we will not let them happen, but that is not healthy. Healthy is recognising them and **acknowledging** them. We are allowed to feel how we feel. It is what we do with them that counts.

R = RELEASE

Yay! It is time to let it all go. This is what it might be like in practice:

What you have written: "I have to work really hard in my business/job..."

Feeling: Mine used to be that I would have a hard menopause like my mother. She really suffered with it. That brings up a sense of anxiety in my tummy. It makes me feel worried that I will not be able to do the other things that I want to do.

(You can write the feeling if you want, or just feel into it – if you can. I often must 'think' into it, but I do know if I think about the issue, it does bring up sensation/feeling for me).

Express: I have to work really hard to succeed in my business – say this statement out loud.

Acknowledge: Say, "Thank you for bringing this fear to my attention. I acknowledge you" (your mind is trying to protect you by bringing up this fear), acknowledge that this is how you feel. It is okay for you to feel that way.

Release: I choose to release you now. Cross it off the list. You can even say 'Rubbish' or 'Nonsense' or whatever word works for you. Mine's a bit stronger to be fair! Release any power the fear has over you. It is SO freeing!

Sometimes they do not come back, but I have found that sometimes they will still be there which is where we can dig a bit more. So, we will be adding another layer to take this even deeper, but for now just get into this practice daily.

Mind Your Language

What you tell yourself is a massive part of getting stuck. Now, I want you to really focus on your self-talk and to start correcting it. Below is a table sharing some common negative patterns.

When you find yourself using these negative patterns, I want you to ask yourself the questions on the right instead. Journal what comes up for you too, and then use the F.E.A.R exercise to clear that stuff out. You are going through enough; you do not need this stuff dragging you down.

 Action

Want to take it one step further? Put a rubber band on your wrist, and every time you say something you know you should not say to yourself, snap that band. It is incredible how quickly you will start to get much better with your language.

NEGATIVE PATTERNS	ASK YOURSELF THIS...
So and so is judging me.	How do I know?
People will think I am... (not at the top of my game, incompetent...)	Can I absolutely know that is true?
	What if the opposite were true?
People will think I am putting out rubbish work.	
You are mind reading!	
It is bad to tell people how you feel.	Who says it is bad?
It is not right asking for support.	How do I know it is not right?
You are making value judgements!	According to whom?
I never get a promotion/the good work/new clients.	Never?
	Really?
I never know what to say.	Nobody?
People never give me good opportunities.	What would happen if they did?
You are giving yourself no choices!	
I should not.	What would happen if I did?
I must not.	What would happen if I did not?
These are really hard words; you are putting hard energy out there!	

I am scared.	Scared of what specifically? (Dig deep on this one)
I am uncomfortable doing...	
Get specific!	What specifically about X makes me feel uncomfortable?
They do not like what I share.	Who specifically does not like what I share?
	Who does not listen to me?
They do not listen to me.	
	Who does not like my contributions?
They do not like my contributions.	
Who is 'they'?	
She is better at X than I am.	Better at what?
He/she is better at doing X.	Compared to what?
Stop comparing. You might be comparing bananas to socks. (As in not comparing like for like)	

At the end of the week, notice any a-ha moments you experienced because of this exercise. It could be enlightening.

What Ruby's husband, Ian, says about menopause

I asked my hubby what his thoughts were around my menopause. The number one thing he came up with (no surprise here, girls) was around sex. I will not go into the details because I am a bit of prude and like to keep my private life, well private. Let us suffice to say that I thought he would mention other things such as how me going through menopause was affecting him, but typically he only had one thing on his mind, which was quite a relief really!

In fairness to him, it was not just about the sex. (*So sorry to my three girls if you are reading this, you never want to hear about your parents' sex life. Do not worry though, you won't be!*)

He just said he does not understand why I do not go on to HRT, as that could resolve all my symptoms. However, I have decided that I want to do this menopause naturally. Thanks to my brilliant medical herbalist, Benn Abdy-Collins, I have significantly reduced my symptoms. I prefer to go through menopause now than to put it off through H.R.T and then go through it in later years. That is my theory anyway. It is a very personal choice, so you must figure out what is right for you.

If you'd prefer not to write in your book, like us, you can download our lovely Reflective Workbook that contains all of the questions we've asked you in one place. Find out more in Chapter 12, Reflective Workbook.

8

OWN YOUR TIME

Timeboxing

Timeboxing is a well-known time management tool. "Individuals can use timeboxing for personal tasks, as well. This technique utilises a reduced scale of time (e.g., 30 minutes instead of a week) and deliverables (e.g., chores instead of a business project component).

Personal timeboxing is said to help curb perfectionist tendencies (by setting a firm time and not overcommitting to a task). Adam Pash writes that timeboxing helps overcome procrastination and that many people find that the time pressure created boosts creativity and focus.

The way I love to do timeboxing is to work with what is called the Pomodoro Technique. Paul Cirello devised this technique. There is a book of the same name that is worth a read.

The concept is simple:

1. You set a timer for 25 minutes
2. In those 25 minutes, you focus on one task
3. Once you finish that task, you take a 5-minute break
4. This completes one block
5. You repeat this cycle for another three blocks
6. At the end of the three blocks, you take a 15-minute break.

To make this effective, you want to have a little plan:

- Set a clear desired outcome
- Chunk the overall goal into mini-goals
- Set a time frame for overall goal*
- Set some milestone dates and rewards for mini goals
- Just do it!

* A little note here - 25-minute blocks are not for everyone. You might feel that the length of time is too long or too short. Set a timeframe that works for you. I have one friend who works in 15-minute blocks, another who works in 45-minute blocks, and another friend who must work in blocks of 2 to 4-hours to be effective.

> 'Productivity is never an accident. It is always the result of a commitment to excellence, intelligent planning, and focused effort'.
>
> *PAUL J MEYER*

When you use this concept, you will be blown away by how much you can achieve.

Manage your Time

Minimise the Fog

How often do you find yourself being pulled from pillar to post while aiming to get essential things done in your working day?

Picture this. You have an important report to complete. Your boss is pushing you to get it ready for a last-minute meeting in half an hour. You start working on the final figures. Then, an urgent email arrives from another department which requires an immediate response. You begin to feel anxious and stressed. Which one takes priority? Suddenly you feel a hot flush coming on. Your mind is under pressure, and your body is on fire. HELP!

Recognise This Scenario?

Working in a high-pressure environment combined with intermittent perimenopause or menopause symptoms can be challenging for women. At times, the act of being able to think straight, to assess and respond to a situation in a calm manner, can feel out of reach and unachievable. Feeling stressed about deadlines and expectations can be overwhelming. The heat rises, mentally and physically, and the pressure mounts.

One of our interviewees, Delia, shares her personal experience of a boardroom moment:

On occasion, I have been right in the middle of an important meeting, and whoosh in comes a hot flush.

I am amazed at how much these flushes can affect how I feel. Perhaps it is because there is no warning, and you try hard to hide the fact. I wish I had the confidence to say, "Excuse me. I am having my own personal summer here. Do you mind if I step out of the room to cool down a bit?"

More often these days, during a meeting, I find it difficult to hold a thought and find myself thinking, what was the question, what was I talking about, or where was I going with this? Experiencing bouts of brain fog means I need to work even harder to keep alert and present. It can be quite tiring doing that."

Women, we say to you, we hear you. We, too, have experienced these momentary lapses in crystal clear laser-focus together with seriously soggy sweats!

As we are here to help you when the heat is on, to reduce and alleviate the impact of perimenopausal or menopausal symptoms, here is a proven method you can try.

It is called *The Power Hour.*

Did you know up to 80% of the average working day is spent on activities with little or no value?

This means that most people only spend 20% of their working day on tasks considered 'important'. Tasks most responsible for wasted time include repeated phone calls due to missed information or – specifically for managers – interruptions as much as 3 hours per working day.

(Source: Cornerstone Dynamics)

Let me shed light on the background of the concept.

Through my career as a performance coach, I have learned about and used many different types of productivity tools. Looking back, I wish I had knowledge of these helpful techniques when I was employed in the corporate world. Work may have been, let's say, more streamlined and easier.

The various tools I have tried and tested have enabled both my work, and my clients' work, to be focused, distraction-free, in flow, and during productive best work hours, which has led to positive and sustainable habits for success.

GOLDEN RULE: To achieve success from the Power Hour, as a solo worker or as a team, it is vital to create boundaries. From client experience, the process works most effectively when

you and your team respect the hour set aside to get focused work completed.

Establish ground rules such as:

- No email response for the next hour
- All mobile phones switched to silent and stored away from the working area, calls (if possible) diverted to answer service
- Put up a visible sign on your chair or office door saying 'No interruptions during my Power Hour (time from and to). Please respect my time'.

Let us get started. Here is *my version* of the Power Hour.

My Power Hour is split into 4 blocks of time: 5 + 40 + 5 + 10 = 60 minutes:

1. **PLAN:** The first 5 minutes is your planning time, where you can write down ONE priority/urgent task to complete in the next 40 minutes
2. **ACTION:** For 40-minutes, you work ONLY on your ONE task, distraction, and interruption-free (this is where boundaries need to be set – more in a moment)
3. **MOVE:** Once your 40-minutes is finished (use a timer – preferably a physical one to avoid looking at your mobile phone), move away from your desk. Make yourself a coffee but avoid interrupting any

colleagues who are on task in a Power Hour –
respect their time

4. **REFLECT:** Spend the last 10 minutes of the
hour reviewing and refining your task.

When you set boundaries and embed the Power Hour into
your work routine, you not only commit to completing
urgent/priority work done, but you also begin a process of
change in mindset and habits toward working smarter, not
harder.

Embed and repeat this process throughout your productive
best/ideal peak work time. Visualise the big personal
reward at the end of each day and week. Imagine how
much more you will achieve.

Make NOW the time to smash your goals without breaking
a sweat!

Be Accountable

Your Secret Weapon to Sustaining Success

Now that you have a super productivity tool to power
through your tasks, you are on the road to victory. However,
while you are enjoying the good vibes of the open road,
with the windows down and a cooling breeze on your skin,
what happens when a sudden obstacle appears? Will your
sweats make you feel stressed, fog make you forgetful, or
your energy wane?

How will you stay cool in the face of a challenge without letting your Power Hour habit slip away?

Enter an accountability partner.

Accountability is a key driver in the continued success of my business for myself and my clients.

Through my work as a performance coach, I have helped many business and corporate leaders adopt and master the vital self-leadership skill of accountability. When clients embrace the power of accountability, the rewards are visible.

It is important to remember; accountability is a process.

As with learning any new skill, becoming responsible takes time to acknowledge and accept your mindset, and embed as a positive routine in your work. Once you realise and accept the value of accountability, you will ultimately become more purpose-driven, effective, and deliver your personal best by living the process and achieving winning results.

Accountability is a support mechanism to enable you to embed, practice and master habits. What do you think happens when you are left to your own devices while strengthening your mindset and trying out techniques? Chances are you are likely to languish as you flounder, trying to keep your head above the water. On the other hand, what do you think happens when you are held accountable for the time, energy and focus you dedicate to a productivity tool like the Power Hour? In my experience, the complete opposite. You are more inclined to want to achieve your tasks for yourself and your accountability partner. You want to feel a sense of accomplishment.

When you engage with an accountability partner, here are the benefits you can anticipate:

Better Focus. You become more targeted, purpose-driven, and productive; as you devote more effort into working toward and reaching your goals. You will be inspired to say, "I achieved X & Y this month" instead of "I did not get much done since we last spoke".

Keep on Track. How often do your ideas lead you down several different paths however, in reality most of them lead nowhere? One idea, one focus, one call, regularly = Winning Results. My clients find that setting one priority action per call encourages them to commit and complete the task. One action can be part of a quarterly set of actions. The process of achieving the complete action plan is broken into manageable and measurable chunks.

Challenge Your Thinking. Having a partner to keep you accountable keeps you grounded. Do you have a habit of talking yourself out of doing complex tasks? Do you permit distractions to zap your energy and focus? Find a partner who will challenge you to consider your options, be real about your intentions, and support you with a timely nudge to shift your mindset from non-finisher to strong finisher.

Increase Momentum. When you meet regularly, momentum happens. Natural flow becomes second nature and together you get things done.

Make Progress. With support, you can ignite limitless thinking to push each other beyond what is possible. Together you focus on how to make sustainable progress happen. Stretch your intentions, focus on what matters most and is a priority, and level up your achievements.

Banish Excuses. Do you get stuck in your thinking, and as a result, nothing happens? Inertia sets in, and time runs away. Your partner will help you push through these blocks to keep you moving forward. Self-built walls and hurdles will fall, enabling you to celebrate your results.

Keep It Real. When we lose sight of why we are doing what we are doing, the situation can get out of control. Focus your partnership on building a strong and supportive connection, keep a check on realistic expectations, listen deeply and be present for each other. Stuck on a challenge? Talk it through, overcome your setback, and move on.

When you choose to act responsibly, and nurture the relationship you build, an accountability partnership will become your greatest asset.

As you can see, when you embrace and build accountability as a positive and progressive practice in your organisation, it is about so much more than staying on track to meet your Power Hour commitments.

Together you can develop sustainable habits for individuals, teams, and the company.

It is all about taking small steps toward building new and effective habits, which lead to efficient work practices, energised distraction-free work focus, engaged people, productive best, and extraordinary performance.

If you'd prefer not to write in your book, like us, you can download our lovely Reflective Workbook that contains all of the questions we've asked you in one place. Find out more in Chapter 12, Reflective Workbook.

9

MANAGE YOUR TIME

How to Think Yourself into Being More Productive

When you sit down at your desk each day, what do you think about first?

- What do you need to achieve for the day?
- Wonder what your connections are up to on social media?
- Avoid facing the tasks you do not want to do?

As you ponder, are your thoughts cheerful, pleasing, and progressive, or are you focussing on the negative, nuisance and non-productive things?

You have a choice as to which type of thought you lead with.

Consider how you feel about yourself and the work you do.

Do you:

- Think positively about the tasks you must complete?
- Focus on achieving your daily goal?
- Look forward to how you will celebrate each small win throughout your day?

When you only focus on how you will feel when you reach your goal, you will miss out on the enjoyment of the process of making your goal happen.

Consider your task list. Which task on your list starts you thinking negatively and can lead you toward a state of procrastination?

What does the process to reach your goal inspire in you? Joy or difficulty?

If you choose Joy, then crack on and make your goal happen.

If you choose Difficulty, then your challenge is to break down the negativity associated with the process.

Are you solely responsible for the process, or can someone else help you?

What is it that you dislike about the journey to the goal?

Is it:

- The time it will take to complete
- The actual work involved (Best use of your skills/talent?)

Think through the process to allow yourself to determine whether the task is yours alone to complete. This will help you clarify the purpose and the importance of your end goal.

Focus on the positive purpose of your goal and its process as you start working toward achieving more.

Choose to think yourself into becoming more productive, in mind and action.

Shift the Fog and Get Your Best Work Done

During menopause, many women in corporate roles feel like they are often in a state of uncontrollable chaos. However, prior to this life phase, the actions of setting goals, making plans, being present and effective in meetings, leading teams, and coping with change in the work environment, were part and parcel of an average working day, week, month, and year. Typically, women could view and deal with these tasks as problem-free and achievable, resulting in positive outcomes.

Enter menopause and its erratic and disruptive nature.

Almost overnight, the way women had to address and process the simplest of tasks was impacted by fluctuating hormones, peaks and troughs in energy levels, intermittent brain fog and sweats, and more. At intervals, these disruptors affected mindset, emotions, and body by 'stealing' the ability to deliver a 'normal' approach to everyday work practices. Corporate women started to notice immediate challenges in their workday, such as the inability to consistently be on their 'A' game, the frequent inability to fire a quick answer or think on the fly in response to a difficult question during a meeting. On top of that, having a complete mind blank of what was discussed in a meeting, and forgetting what actions must be completed.

Sound familiar?

Let us face the reality of the situation. Menopause is a phase in life that most women experience. In tandem, with a corporate career, women who go through this phase want to do so with as minimal impact as possible, right?

Unfortunately, there is no magic wand to wave or wish to grant that you will experience *no* menopausal symptoms during work hours.

Instead, an ideal and helpful way to alleviate the state of uncontrollable chaos and reduce the impact of these disruptors is to take control of the way you think, act, and do.

In other words, how you manage your mindset. When you take this positive approach, you present yourself with an opportunity to not just struggle and survive through your menopause experience. Instead, you can take back control, power up your mindset, continue to thrive in your role, and regain the ability to deliver your 'A' game consistently.

How *much* do you want to remain effective in your role, maintain your energy, and deliver your productive best?

The first step is to develop and strengthen your mindset. Your mindset is the most powerful tool you have at your disposal. The right mindset, teamed with proven tools and techniques, can help you better manage menopause in the work environment.

Ready to take back control?

Let us start with the 'usual suspects' or main disruptors in the workplace that prove to be frequently impacted by menopausal symptoms. These include:

- Last-minute team meetings/reports
- Ping pong email trails
- Unrealistic expectations (self and company)
- Lack of direction
- Unsupportive environment.

Alone these disruptors may cause chaos in mindset without the influence of menopausal symptoms. However, with symptoms, the level of impact tends to become heightened.

Before sharing mindset hacks you can implement, let us look at Lin's menopause experience:

"Basically, I did not feel I was being my most effective self. I was busy working full-time in an incredibly demanding corporate job with multiple targets, with clients and staff who were all looking to me for direction. At times, I felt like I was in a fog.

On many occasions, I felt like I was back-pedalling when trying to clarify and communicate my thoughts. In effect, working twice as hard to get the same results. It just felt like a major personal challenge to not feel as effective or be on my 'A' game. Sometimes it was difficult to complete even the simplest task.

Losing thought processes and concentration, and feeling lethargic by the afternoon, was like I had just run out of steam."

From Lin's story, it is evident how her reduced ability to complete tasks and lead effectively showed up in her work. She struggled against the expectations she set for herself and those expected within the organisation, together with brain fog and lethargy. This is where mindset comes into play and how we manage the feelings and thoughts we have.

Faced with the challenge of how to win through, what do you feel is the best approach for Lin to take back control of her mindset?

Here is Lin's plan of action:

"I discovered I was more productive in the morning, so I focused on completing priority tasks during this time. I

allowed myself extra time to complete work and arrive earlier at meetings, not as a last-minute rush. Rushing caused bigger problems. When I gave myself extra time to write notes and prepare, it did lengthen the process. However, by doing so, I felt happier, more in control, and was able to communicate my message with clarity and efficiency.

After meetings, I made time to reflect on the discussion and any notes I made, which helped when emailing follow up memos and planning future meetings with my team. Without my post-meeting routine, my plans would have been 'stolen' and 'lost' because of moments of brain fog and forgetfulness.

Concentration and attention to detail is something I pride myself on. During menopause, my focus wavered on occasion. However, having a focused to-do list kept me on track. I was more productive because I completed tasks, tracked my progress, and managed to be less overwhelmed when meetings were rescheduled, or changes of task were required."

What will you take away from Lin's approach?

From Lin's experience here are three mindset hacks you can try to manage your mindset and menopause better:

1. Productive Best. Discover the ideal time in your working day when you deliver your best work. Even in a corporate environment, you can choose to focus on and deliver your best work at an optimum time for you holistically, in mind, body and self. If you, like Lin, are at your productive best in the morning, maximise this time for priority work. My productive best hours are 9.00am to 1.00pm. This time is sacred, focused work time. I choose to dedicate my morning hours to being creative and writing. Over time, my productive best time has become a positive and rewarding success habit.

In a leadership role? Help your team discover their productive best work time to maximise the energy and output for the team and company. Be a role model for mindset and build efficiency in individuals, teams, and the organisation.

2. Plan. Make time or give yourself extra time to plan for upcoming meetings, reports to be completed, and for follow up. Block time in your diary (and protect it) to build a positive and progressive habit. Create a daily Success List to ignite your mindset to focus on (and to reduce forgetfulness from brain fog) completing priority/urgent/most important tasks. Think about what the Success List says to you. Consider viewing it as a positive prompt to help you accomplish great things and achieve winning results.

3. Realistic Expectations. When you set high expectations for yourself at work whilst experiencing the challenges of menopause, you allow chaos to reign. Why fight with yourself and your struggles and believe you must push yourself to meet all the demands of work and your physical or emotional fluctuations? Instead, be kind to yourself and adopt a gentler pace to your working day. Integrate realistic expectations within your planning and productive best work times. Role model your expectation approach with your team to encourage better personal and work practices.

Shift your mindset from chaos to clarity. Accept and acknowledge how, when and what triggers your menopause symptoms. Take control of your mindset as an effective approach to help you better manage menopause in life, career and business. Then, plan for success, deliver your productive best, fuel personal fulfilment, and achieve fruitful outcomes.

It is time to banish the fog and get your best work done!

20 Ways to Beat Procrastination

Let's face it, you, me, we all procrastinate.

When faced with a task, we often question, think, and decide whether to do something or not. As a result, many procrastinators find themselves frequently asking: Shall I do it now or later?

Interestingly, there are pros and cons for procrastination.

An often-associated con is that procrastination can lead to stagnation and inaction. In choosing to not act on this behaviour, an individual fails to move in any direction. Contributing factors that may compound the level of procrastination can include overthinking, over-burdened workload, lack of clarity, focus and direction, and mindset.

On the flip-side, as a pro, procrastination can become a creative and progressive action. In this instance, an individual will pause and review a task at hand with a creative perspective. This approach eliminates a forced knee-jerk reaction just because a specific job needs to be completed.

Be mindful that too much procrastination regularly can sap both energy and confidence in who you are and what you do. Like the outcome of inaction, where nothing happens, so too, when you lack confidence, you feel less inclined to motivate and boost yourself and the work you deliver.

Here are 20 tips to help you better manage your mindset and the way you approach procrastination:

1. Write only three priority, urgent, important tasks on your Success List each morning. Complete each task: 1, 2, 3 and then list your next three tasks. Focus on 'waltzing' your way effectively through your day
2. What can you delete from your to-do list that is diminishes rather than multiplying your focus and energy?
3. Spend 10 minutes of focus on breaking big tasks into smaller chunks of time to allow you to focus on one thing at a time
4. Complete the 5-Minute Miracle. 1) What action can I take in less than 5 minutes today that moves my task forward even the tiniest bit? 2) Set a timer for 5 minutes and work on the task

5. Be kind to yourself. Avoid beating yourself up in your quest to aim for perfection or to meet unrealistic expectations

6. Be mindful. When you think negative thoughts such as fear of failure, shake your head

7. Build the positive habit of a Power Hour into your daily workflow. Success tip: ONE TASK = ONE POWER HOUR. (5 minutes planning, 40 minutes action on a task, 5 minutes move away from your desk to refresh your thoughts, 10 minutes reflect and polish) REPEAT

8. Block on-task time in your diary and protect it at all costs. How much time will you allocate per task (link to getting it done during your Power Hour)

9. Stop and ask yourself three questions – Where are you? What do you want to do? How will you feel after doing it?

10. Set deadlines to make a task/project concrete in your mind

11. Forgive your past attempts to overcome inaction because of cluttered, negative thoughts. Start with a clean slate and switch your mindset to focus on: "What can go RIGHT?"

12. Play your favourite power song as a pep talk and inspiration to get started

13. Explore the questions you ask yourself about your Why attached to the task ahead. Is the outcome led by a 'Have to' or 'Want to' goal?

14. Go for a walk and stop thinking about the task. Gift yourself a burst of fresh air for greater clarity, focus and ignite action
15. Stop talking and Do It. Act NOW and let the natural flow of results happen
16. Focus on starting instead of finishing. When you visualise the first step and ask yourself: "What can I do right now?" you create momentum. Action takes place, and you will get things done
17. Make the task FUN. What can you do once it is complete? What is your reward?
18. Gift yourself a BONUS. Remember to celebrate the small wins
19. Breathe. Close your eyes and focus on your breathing for 5 minutes
20. Be accountable. Find an accountability partner who will challenge, motivate, and inspire you to rise to the task and deliver your best work.

Remember – the best way to get something done is to begin!

What other tips do you find helpful to eliminate or embrace procrastination to achieve sustainable, winning results?

The Chicken Story

Next, let us talk chickens!!

Let me share ...

I now live in Scotland, having moved up from England a few years ago. As we move into autumn, the weather can get a bit wet, wild, and windy. So much so, they even have a name for this type of weather up here. It is called 'dreich' (pronounced 'dreek.')

We have a few chickens, and on a particular dreich October day, our chickens were having trouble figuring out how to get up the ladder of their new home so that they could put themselves to bed. So I spent ages outside getting soaked from head to foot, trying to help them to understand that they needed to climb the little ladder to get to bed.

Fast forward 24-hours, and I decided that I was not going to have a repeat experience, and I thought I would 'bribe' my lovely girls into bed with one of their favourites now and again treats - a tiny piece of cheese.

Instead of letting them get up the steps themselves, I decided that I would put them through the nesting box so that they could get to their perch a bit quicker, and I would not get soaked again. So I quickly got all of them happily to bed, shut the door and went indoors, a little bit less wet than the day before, not much though!

A few moments later, I was standing in the kitchen, drying myself off, when I heard a noise at the back door that sounded like a chicken. Sure enough, it was one of the girls. She was sitting on the back doorstep. Hilariously, what had happened was as I was moving them through the side nesting box, they were coming out the other end because I had not shut the door!! Now whether this was because of menopause or not, who knows? However, it is a good example of how forgetful you can be with menopause brain fog, so Gail thought it would be a great idea to pop it in the book anyway!

We would love to hear your brain fog stories. Email us, our contact information is at the back of the book.

Radical Focus

Radical focus is that place where nothing else matters because you are focused on -

One. Single. Thing.

We are overwhelmed by information overload, both on and offline. Think how complicated it can be these days even to order a simple cup of coffee!

We can easily bring back control by deciding to practice radical focus, making our time count.

This level of focus is not a new phenomenon, but once you start practising radical focus, you will be amazed at how much work you will get through in a short space of time.

Here are three top tips on how to get radical focus:

1. Notice Your Time Distractions

Where is your time going? Once you know, you are much better able to manage it. It is not about working harder but about being smart and savvy with your time.

2. Work in Time Blocks and Focus on ONE Thing

Sometimes getting started is the hardest part. Work in time blocks. The concept is simple, set a timer, and before you start, set a very clear goal about what you want to achieve in that time block. Then go and do it!

This is where the Pomodoro Technique will really help you.

3. Set Yourself Up for Success

Create the right environment and set clear boundaries so that you cannot be disturbed. You could even create a focus playlist. Neuroscientists tell us that our brains connect with different anchors. Music can be a powerful anchor.

Radical focus is a gift you can give to yourself. It is simple but not easy. All it takes is a bit of thought and a lot of discipline.

Success Habits

When you are going through menopause, you need to put things in place that can support you in creating success.

If you are anything like some of the women we have been speaking to, you may find there are times when your brain does not seem to function as well as usual. Other times it will be like you are on steroids. Either way, if you can set some success habits you will give yourself the greatest chance of being productive on days when it is just not happening.

As we have shared, one great way to start your day is to have a morning routine. This routine can be comprised of lots of micro habits that, over time can create massive change. You will more than likely have heard the metaphor around an aeroplane changing course. If the pilot sets the path to change by 1°, over time, the plane will end up in a completely different location to that originally intended. The same can apply to your habits. They might seem simple now; however, each of these micro habits that you put into place will make a difference.

As we only have a finite amount of willpower, creating a routine can help us stay the course. When you do not have to think about what you need to do and create a routine around it, you are far more likely to complete them.

Many years ago, I came across a behaviour scientist, and author called B J Fogg. He created the Fogg Behaviour Model, which is this:

B=MAP

Here is how he explains it: "Behaviour (B) happens when Motivation (M), Ability (A), and a Prompt (P) come together at the same moment."

When I think about my clients, most of them are highly motivated. They can do the tasks they set themselves. They sometimes just need the prompt or trigger to get them going. Unfortunately, menopause can stand in the way of that motivation, so sometimes it needs a bit of help.

When I first came across BJ Fogg (*no menopausal brain fog pun intended!*), he talked about triggers where you have something that triggers you to undertake that task. For example, if you want to go to the gym, put your gym bag by the front door. The presence of the bag is more likely to trigger you into going to the gym, as it is ready and waiting for you.

You might find yourself resisting the very idea of creating a routine. However, you are probably already doing one. What is the first thing that you do when you get out of bed? It is likely that you will follow several micro habits without even thinking. For example, you might take yourself to the kitchen to make a cup of tea or coffee, grab a bite to eat, then go back up and brush your teeth, make your bed, and get ready to start your working day.

S J Scott, author of Habit Stacking: 97 Small Life Changes That Take Five Minutes or Less, suggests that you create a list of habits that you stack up, then attach a reason to each of those habits.

If you check out any successful leaders, both corporate and Queens of Biz, you will find that there is a common theme of habits they share that have created their success:

1. **They look after their wellbeing** - through good sleep, nutrition, exercise
2. **They learn** - they are constantly developing their strengths through reading and learning
3. **They focus on tasks that are 'action producing money'**. They do not waste time on low-end tasks that do not give them a return for their investment of time
4. **They set big goals** and then break them down into smaller manageable chunks

5. **They protect their time -** by setting boundaries
6. **They focus -** they choose to zone in on tasks and take them through to completion. They are finishers
7. **They set routines** - They may sound boring, but they are necessary, especially when you have brain fog.

Neuroscience tells us that we can change the way our brains think by implementing habits. An article by Bri Flynn Withhuhn on Forbes shared that researchers at Duke University found that more than 40% of our actions each day are based on habit rather than conscious thought. 40%. So, if we are running on autopilot, then let us make that 40% count.

What habits could you create for your success?

Now for the full interviews. Here are the stories from some incredible women who have shared their personal stories so that you can learn different ways to manage your menopause while you work.

We hope you agree that these women are all amazing. We are pleased that people are now talking about menopause more openly, and we appreciate these women so much for being brave enough to share their stories with you and us. Our hope is that you learn some valuable tips from their stories that you can apply to your life today.

If you'd prefer not to write in your book, like us, you can download our lovely Reflective Workbook that contains all of the questions we've asked you in one place. Find out more in Chapter 12, Reflective Workbook.

10

REAL LIFE STORIES

Debbie's Story

How did menopause affect you in your working life?

I have identified three key areas of impact.

The first impact, I believe, is one that most women can relate to, a lack of concentration, often described as the fog. The problem is it took a while for me to relate the symptom to menopause. I just thought I was too busy or tired. What I did not quite realise, until having come through menopause, was that this was a very significant symptom, one that made me start to question my performance.

As someone who is generally very focused, I typically have good conversations without even thinking about having good conversations. They just flow. Suddenly I thought, "What is going on? What am I saying? This throws the second impact in, this heightened emotional state which has a huge impact on the way you behave.

I started to feel overly emotional about things I previously would never have felt emotional about. The fog and my emotions made it quite hard to manage because, when I was going through menopause, I was becoming quite dissatisfied with my work environment.

As I reflect on the way I managed my exit from the role at that time, it was embarrassing. I was just so emotional, and I took things so personally. It was absolutely around all this time that the third impact hit – the disturbed sleep.

Let me paint a picture. I was tired. My energy level was low. My emotions were heightened, and I was wading through a fog. Time bombed.

What do you think was the biggest challenge for you?

I think the biggest challenge was I did not realise the length of time menopause could last. I remember going to see a GP because I decided I was not going on HRT. Instead, I would go through the experience. In hindsight I am so pleased I made that decision, because as my GP informed me, menopause can be a five-to-ten-year process. Other women I know have been faced with the same question, what do I do to manage menopause, especially as they have concerns about breast cancer and osteoporosis.

Had I known more at the start of the process, I could have handled things differently. When someone tells you

'Menopause is going to take a while', you know straight away you can expect different symptoms at different stages. Menopause becomes a way of life, so you get used to good days, bad days, and better days.

During menopause, I was Mum to two senior teenage daughters and a wife to a husband with a highly stressful job. A tough challenge to say the least. An interesting time in my life.

What did you do to manage and cope with the symptoms we have discussed and the challenges you faced?

I felt fortunate to have a close inner circle of women friends with whom I could touch base and share symptoms. You know, often we would laugh about our experiences, we would make jokes, and we might cry together. So, having a female support network with women who are going through a similar experience, well, there is nothing better. You know it is like the midwife who turns around and says, "just go to sleep" while you are having contractions. Clearly, she has never given birth in her life. Honestly, my circle of friends was great.

The other thing I did was to make time to get away and create my own space, to detach myself when I was feeling really fed up or emotional. Time and space allowed me a chance to work through what I was feeling. Sometimes I would go for a walk or upstairs and lay down on the bed and read a book, just to calm down.

What one piece of advice can you share for women who are going through the same experience or similar?

Do your research on symptom management. Being an optimist, I breezed through menopause, going ahead and getting on with it. Jump forward to now, and I know there is plenty of brilliant research available, particularly related to nutritional advice. If I had my experience again, I would have worked with a nutritionist.

Have an open and honest conversation with those closest to you who are most impacted by the changes in your behaviour. Sit down together and explain what you are going through, why you are behaving differently, and how the family can support you when you are tired or emotional.

I feel we need to talk more about menopause, especially in the workplace. Like the conversation with your family, the same applies in the workplace. It is about awareness, acceptance, honesty, respect, and support for all leaders and teams. Through open communication, your colleagues can learn to understand the process and how productivity levels for women going through menopause may be different.

Occupational health can play a huge role in supporting women because menopause can be a ten-year journey. For women who start menopause at 50 years of age, the phase may continue right up to retirement. For them, this is the last big chunk of their working life. These women want to remember this period as a time where they delivered impact, influence and benefited from personal growth. If women in the workplace remain challenged by the emotional turmoil associated with menopause in an unsupportive space, their final years of employment may leave them feeling undervalued and disappointed.

Delia's Story

Her Memorable Moment: *I was presenting to a potential investor – who shall remain nameless – and had been practising my pitch for ages and thinking through all the possible questions that could come up. I was mid-pitch, it was going well, and then brain fog hit. My mind went completely blank mid-sentence. I could almost "see" the fog it was so thick! I thought it unlikely the guy would understand that I was having a menopausal moment, so I literally had to bluff it. We did not get the investment – COVID hit, and their investment strategy changed – but I will always wonder whether he noticed or whether I managed to pull off the bluff... Thanks, menopause, for that uncomfortable moment!*

How is menopause affecting you in your work life?

To disclose upfront, I am in the perimenopause phase. For me there are three definite menopause factors taking place in my life: brain fog, hot flushes, and weight gain.

Brain fog is like wading through treacle where I am literally struggling to power up my brain. At other times, when I attempt to hold onto a concept or idea without letting it slip away, it is like trying to hold a bar of soap in the shower. That is how I can best define brain fog.

Next is hot flushes. I tend to experience flushes in the morning. This is frustrating because I have just had my shower and sorted myself for the day ahead. Lo and behold, next minute, I am having my own personal summer. Hot flushes are not exclusive to mornings. While on a packed train on my way to a meeting, or right in the middle of an important meeting, and whoosh in comes a hot flush.

I am amazed at how much these flushes can affect how I feel. Perhaps it is because there is no warning, and you try hard to hide the fact. I wish I had the confidence to say, "Excuse me. I am having my own personal summer here. Do you mind if I step out of the room to cool down a bit?"

Lastly is weight gain. When you are feeling menopausal, it is not fun going to your wardrobe to choose suitable clothes for a business meeting. Suddenly, your favourite outfit is a bit of a tight squeeze. This is not helped by the onset of a hot flush and the feeling that you have thickened around the middle.

Of the three challenges you shared, which one has been the most challenging for you as a professional woman in the corporate world?

It is a toss-up between brain fog and hot flushes. Brain fog because with hot flushes, I find myself saying more often,

"Excuse me, I'm having a hot flush', to make light of my situation. I feel it is slowly becoming more accepted in the workplace; however, a greater level of awareness and acceptance is needed.

With brain fog, it feels like wading through treacle or trying to hold onto something that is slipping away. More often these days, during a meeting, I find it difficult to hold a thought and find myself thinking, what was the question, what was I talking about, or where was I going with this? Experiencing bouts of brain fog means I need to work even harder to keep alert and present. It can be quite tiring doing that.

It is not all negative, though. I have worked out ways to cope with brain fog and hot flushes. Firstly, for hot flushes, I pay more attention to what clothes I wear. It is important to consider the fabric and colours and what might show, such as heavy perspiration. Personally, I choose to wear black or loose layers to counteract and cool myself when required.

For brain fog, I have spent time focusing on what I am eating and how I am exercising. Before, I talked about weight gain during menopause. With exercise, I realised that pounding the pavements and doing miles of running was not necessarily enough or the right thing for me to manage my weight. Now I have switched to a very different regime, more for menopausal women, which focuses on different types of cardio combined with strength exercises.

From a nutrition perspective, I have massively reduced my sugar, carbohydrates, and alcohol intake. I quickly noticed a big difference to my energy levels and the ability to concentrate for longer. As well, I noticed a direct link between alcohol and moments of brain fog. There are countless ways you can try to better cope during this life phase. It feels great to know I have hit upon specific techniques which are helping to make positive changes in my life.

In a corporate setting, how do you prepare yourself for meetings to reduce the impact of any symptoms?

Personally, to keep track of and manage all the things I need to remember to do. I have increased my use of Trello. There are many productivity tools available, and Trello works for me. Capturing what I need to remember helps with being more prepared for meetings. This allows me to focus on what I want to say and the important points I need to get across. Being prepared, with notes in hand, is a confidence booster.

Active listening enables a better level of being present in conversations. When I listen intently, I feel more engaged in a discussion as opposed to allowing a conversation to float over you and rely on chipping in with thoughts. Being more purposeful allows for improved discussions and progressive outcomes.

In my mind, preparation is key. I believe it helps to tune your brain in and to give those neurons a chance to charge up and connect better. A positive, helpful, and repetitive habit to develop.

What is one piece of advice that you could share for women who are going through a similar experience as you?

Share your experience with others. Talk about perimenopause and menopause. When we women talk about our experiences, we often laugh about what we are going through because it is funny. It's frustrating, and somewhat annoying but, the moments are funny.

Be brave and openly communicate your menopause moments with women in your life and work. I am encouraged as more people write articles and books on the topic, which can lead to a positive and progressive opportunity to raise awareness and reduce the taboo label.

We need to reach a place where it will be okay to acknowledge, accept and be more inclusive about menopause in life, business, and career, across the world.

Jenny's Story

How does menopause affect you in your working life?

The toughest thing about menopause is that you do not realise it is going on. You feel different; however, as we are human beings and there is a lot going on in life, you do not know what is driving that change within you.

I guess I felt unprepared.

Being totally honest, I had little knowledge about peri-menopause, what may happen, how to deal with it, or the symptoms. For me, I cannot pinpoint when this phase started.

There is no one physical sign that gives you a head up, apart from when your periods change in frequency. As we now know, there is a whole premenopausal period that is going on; however, it is not clear when that started. First, you start to sense some changes and differences. It is unsettling because you know something is going on, but you are not sure what it is.

I started looking online and listening to podcasts about women who have experienced mild and chronic symptoms.

For some women, who suffer from menopause-related depression, they reach the point of feeling completely overwhelmed or sometimes suicidal.

One of the challenges is not understanding and not knowing what to expect. Even now, when you go online to find information, there is a limited amount available. As a woman, I will go through menopause. However, I feel it is outrageous that many women go through this period by having to 'suck it up and get on with it'. You muddle your way through it, finding out along the way what works for you. This is the approach I have taken. In hindsight, perhaps I could have acknowledged the stage earlier had I been able to access the help and support I needed.

I have now decided to research HRT and make an appointment with the doctor to have a conversation about menopause.

What have you noticed as changes in yourself in terms of when you are working?

Brain fog. A steady slowing down in my response time to take in and understand information. In a way, my thinking is delayed rather than being instantaneous as it was in the past.

From a work perspective, I feel the bigger picture around my delayed thinking time links to feeling and reacting differently. It does slightly knock your confidence because you realise things are shifting, which can be a little unnerving. Around the feeling of change is uncertainty. This can create doubt, and you often feel less than 100% yourself. Maybe the slowness stems from self-questioning as I experience the changes happening.

What is the impact on your productivity at work, now you are experiencing increasing levels of interrupted sleep?

Lack of sleep impacts how you feel the next day, and it slows down your reactions. This becomes another part of the whole circle of things that have an impact on you and shift within you. Not getting enough restful sleep on a regular basis is energy-zapping and a productivity thief. On the flip-side, for me, the power of restorative sleep works wonders, helping me to be at my productive best.

What techniques have you tried to improve your sleep, have more energy, and focus on conversations better?

Being more mindful about what I eat, drink and exercise. I have cut out caffeine after midday, alcohol on weeknights, I consciously eat food that makes me feel good, and getting out for regular exercise. When I live mindfully, I give myself a taste of a healthier lifestyle and great sleep, and I want more of it. I have noticed that good sleep patterns lead to feeling more upbeat, energised, and focused.

What is one valuable piece of advice for women who are going through menopause?

Honestly, I would say, do not sleepwalk into menopause. Be prepared. Ask questions and seek the advice and support you need to be better informed. Keep talking about it – how you are feeling, what you are experiencing, and share the journey with other women.

Start conversations in your early '40s. I wish I had. There needs to be more discussions and support for women in menopause, on a personal and professional level. We need to have more open conversations, together with more research, to support the changing nature of this phase in women's lives.

It is time to remove the shame, the 'taboo' topic of menopause, in the work environment. How many corporate women feel confident to raise their hand and say, 'Today is a brain fog day', or 'I need a little more time to process the conversation we have had, so I can make the right decision?

Menopause is a natural part of a woman's life. Responsible organisations must acknowledge, accept, and empower women going through menopause. Building an inclusive culture of respect and trust, where women and men feel comfortable talking and sharing the experience, is vital.

When we think about women in their '50s who were our managers in the past, some displayed erratic behaviour. Who could they turn to and talk about what they were experiencing? Back then, nobody talked about menopause and the impact it was having on older women in the workplace.

Let us hope, with more education and books like yours, that change in the work environment can take place. Together women and men can talk about menopause equally. Open and honest discussion can help men understand more about the impact of menopause in the workplace and provide women with support, to manage and cope with menopause and continue to participate fully and effectively in their roles.

Have you discovered a window of hours in your workday that enable your peak performance?

With at least seven hours of solid sleep, going through the night without a disturbance, I am happy to get up at 5:00am and work until 1:00pm. This is my ideal working time to complete the things I absolutely want to get done that day. During the afternoon, I focus on work at more of a leisurely pace. Afternoon tasks that do not require the same level of attention or focus.

In the corporate environment, it is not realistic to go to work at 5:00am and finish at 1.00pm. You are expected to be in the office by 8:30am and to work until 5:30pm. So, what do I do to deliver my best work in my productive best hours, as I go through menopause? For me, it is down to having a positive relationship with the team. It is about creating boundaries based on flexibility, acceptance, respect, and open communication.

When I am working on a time-sensitive project, I inform my team and ask to be uninterrupted between certain hours. I let them know that I am available over my lunch hour or later in the day, should someone need to get hold of me. It works. I feel it is important for more organisations to cultivate a culture where acceptance, trust, respect, flexibility, and open communication is the norm. After all, when we work together and help each other deliver our best work, everyone is happy and productive.

Karen's Story

Her Memorable Moment: *Sitting around the fire in the evening with my partner in southern France and having a deep feeling of happiness and contentment: that all was well and nothing missing.*

How did menopause affect you in your working life?

Not very much at all, which I am happy to say. I have experienced hardly any symptoms of menopause, no mood swings, no pains in the body, and minimal hot flushes. My menopause has been very smooth.

What do you think helped you to be able to go through menopause with little impact?

For the last ten years, my periods, when I still had them, were very painful. When I think back to my earlier life, I hardly had any period pains, aches, symptoms, or challenges.

Something changed in my late '30s, early '40s.

From that time onwards, I had extremely heavy periods every month, with very painful aches in my lower back and belly, for the first two days, to the point that I had to take medication. From this experience, I always thought that my menopause time would be equally challenging.

There are a few things I did that helped to minimise the impact of menopause. Firstly, I have always looked after myself well. I enjoy meditation, yoga, walking, cycling, and swimming. I love to do lots of physical exercise in the great outdoors. I eat well, although I have never followed any diets because I believe moderation works best for me.

Practising mindfulness to keep my mind and body in a calm state really helps.

For me, it is about lifestyle, awareness and mindset. Through meditation and mindfulness, I become more aware of the pains, challenges, difficulties, and emotions associated with menopause. I began to see them for what they were, and I knew that they would pass. These feelings were not permanent.

Intuitively when you experience pain, you often push against it, which makes it worse. This adds more pain to the pain already there. It does make a difference when you learn to work with your mind, and you kindly accept the changes you are going through.

Going through menopause acknowledges that we are moving away from fertility and toward a different phase in our life.

An important point to mention is the move into a relationship with ageing. For women, this stage of the ageing process can be difficult. As we transition to the next phase, we need to embrace a relationship with body and hormonal changes and ageing. It is about adapting your lifestyle for what comes next.

Lin's Story

Her Memorable Moment: *You could tap into women in menopause, light up the city and run the country on them. The national grid did well in my world. Lin lights up London!*

How did menopause affect you in your working life?

Basically, I did not feel I was being my most effective self. I was busy working full-time, in an incredibly demanding job with multiple targets, with clients and staff who were all looking to me for direction. At times, I felt like I was in a fog.

On many occasions, I felt like I was backpedalling when trying to clarify and communicate my thoughts. In effect, working twice as hard to just to get the same results. It just felt like a major personal challenge to not feel as effective or be on my 'A' game. Sometimes it was difficult to complete even the simplest task.

Losing thought processes and concentration, and feeling lethargic by the afternoon, was like I had just run out of steam. I discovered I was more productive in the morning, so I focused on completing priority tasks during this time.

What worked for you to manage and cope with your challenges?

Firstly, I allowed myself extra time. Extra time to complete work and arrive earlier at meetings, not as a last-minute rush. Rushing caused bigger problems. When I gave myself extra time to write notes and prepare, it did lengthen the process. However, by doing so, I felt happier, more in control, and was able to communicate my message with clarity and efficiency.

After meetings, I made time to reflect on the discussion and any notes I made, which helped when emailing follow up memos and planning future meetings with my team. Without my post-meeting routine, my plans would have been 'stolen' and 'lost' because of moments of brain fog and forgetfulness.

Concentration and attention to detail is something I pride myself on. During menopause, my focus wavered on occasion. Having a focused To-do list kept me on track. I was more productive because I completed tasks, tracked my progress, and managed to be less overwhelmed when meetings were rescheduled or changes of task were required.

Having a cool shower helped me relax after a busy day. Especially a day filled with a heavy meeting schedule and client appointments. And a good night's sleep too, if possible, depending on the frequency of night sweats. Keeping myself as well, fit and energised as possible helped too.

What advice do you have for professional women who are going through menopause?

Be kind to yourself. Your body and hormones are going into overdrive. If you feel like menopause is controlling you, take charge and find a way to be in control. Each woman will experience something different. Begin to take notice of your hormonal routines - when you are most effective and when you know you are forgetful. Create to-do lists to get your best work done and to reduce the impact of forgetfulness. Buy a small fan to cope with hot flushes. Allow yourself more time to do things, to relieve unnecessary pressure, anxiety, and stress.

In the work environment, it is important that people, women, and men, can talk about menopause because there are few discussions taking place. Raising awareness of the topic can start conversations, build an open and inclusive culture, and have a positive and supportive impact on, not only women going through menopause but across the team and organisation as well.

We live in an age of vulnerability where previously 'taboo' topics like menopause are starting to be discussed. During my mother's era, no one spoke about the subject, not even with their friends. At the time, women experienced menopause in silence.

Today, we see more women in the workplace, with growing numbers in leadership positions and running businesses. Being active in the workspace presents a positive and progressive opportunity for open communication, greater awareness, and empathy.

Find self-care activities that work for you. I enjoyed a mix of Body Balance, Tai Chi, Pilates, and aqua aerobics. These exercises gave me a boost of energy. Walking was a solo activity I loved to do, to get outside and clear my thoughts in a different space.

One final piece of advice: Accept the peaks and troughs of your menopausal experience, your thoughts, feelings, and emotions.

Amanda's Story

Her memorable moment:

Leading a team in a Creative Agency in Switzerland and working with all different cultures, so not your typical English banter office environment. I was working on a UN event, so it was a pressured time. Trying to talk to the team in our stand up meeting, and I remember opening the window and hanging out of it from the waist up over-looking the car park - just thinking I would cool down faster if more of me was out of the window! I just owned it in the end and said, excuse me whilst I'm having a hot flush, carry on amongst yourselves!

How did/does menopause affect you in your working life?

I'm in the perimenopause stage and now looking back, I think it's been going on longer than I realised. I saw a nutritionist who suggested getting a hormone levels test done which confirmed I was in perimenopause. Thankfully, I was living in France at the time, so it was a seamless and efficient process.

The main ways that midlife has affected me are my energy levels, hot flushes, and brain fog. There are many more, but these take the top spots!

Before my day even starts, I must check in with how I'm feeling before I even get out of bed! I could have low energy levels or extreme fatigue - which doesn't even make any sense given I've been asleep, except that it depends on the quality of sleep. Overnight I could have had several trips to the toilet and night sweats or be nursing a headache or migraine.

These symptoms can have an impact on my day, especially working online with clients. I've learnt to dance with the hot flushes if one happens during a client or group session, and I can joke about it, but I still find it embarrassing, especially if it's a particularly sweaty one and the tissues come out to mop up the sweat!

Brain fog is another beast altogether, which is very infuriating. I find myself writing more notes now than I used to, as I know the thought will fall out of my head as quickly as it popped in.

My energy levels are an interesting symptom and an area I've started to experiment with, so things are slowly improving the more I learn about myself, the work I do and the triggers.

I've started working with the moon cycles, as obviously, I have no other monthly cycle to go on. Tapping into mother nature's rhythm has been interesting, eye-opening and a game changer so far in the process. As a result, I now schedule client/group calls during my more energetic weeks and do the work that needs less energy in my not-so energetic weeks.

What was/is the biggest challenge for you?

The biggest challenge in my business is managing the brain fog and hot flushes. Outside of work, I am personally finding it hard to navigate this midlife journey and accept the life stage I'm at - physically, emotionally, and mentally. I still think I can do things that I did 5 or 10 years ago only to find there's a new physical ache or that the activity just doesn't fill me up anymore. I'm also quite young to be going through perimenopause, and a lot of my friends have young children. I have one friend already in menopause, and it's great to be able to have a chinwag with her so we can help and support each other through this journey into midlife.

What worked/works for you to manage/cope?

Diet:

To help reduce the number of hot flushes I have, I only drink water now when I'm working. If I drink tea or a hot drink, I must think about the timing of it!

I'm starting to track my symptoms and see if there's any link to the foods I eat. I try to avoid sugar and spicy food and save alcohol for the weekends. It doesn't always happen, though, in which case it's a choice to make. Eat or drink it and accept the symptoms or not!

Health & Exercise:

I get outside and walk every single day to get my 10k steps in. I also cycle, swim and attend Pilates regularly. I sometimes dance to a 3-minute music track just to move my body. It's a great excuse to show off those midlife dance moves too!

Stress is a trigger for menopause symptoms, so I make sure I try and bring in as much play, fun and laughs into my day. I even tried laughing yoga on Friday lunchtime!

Meditation once a day, sometimes twice if I'm feeling pressured, and the call to be grounded also really helps.

Morning routine

Having my morning routine helps before starting work. Having a schedule with my working blocks keeps me productive. Benchmarks in my day help to incorporate habits and stick to them. All of these can make or break a good day for me, so it does make a huge difference.

During my lower energy weeks, I may change up my environment to work as well depending on energy levels - sometimes sitting at my desk trying to force it at the wrong time can feel draining and instinctively, I know it's not right, so it's time to walk away or change things.

Alternative supplements

I'm trying a lot of alternative medicine at the moment and putting off taking HRT. For my low mood and irritability, I take 5HTP, which releases serotonin. I take supplements (menohop) specifically for menopause.

If you could share one piece of advice for women going through the same, what would it be?

Experiment with your diet and supplements

Adjust your diet to help work with the changes going on in your body. Monitor your symptoms and see if you can spot any triggers related to what you ate the day before, and experiment by cutting it out of your diet. This is also the same for supplements. Not all of them work with your body, so you must experiment a bit.

Practical steps with your work life:

Keep a fan and tissues on your desk, and make sure you get away from your desk to move your body and exercise every day, even if it's a 20-minute walk!

Now more than ever, you need to treat yourself to kindness and self-love and take time off! Look after your health.

Be realistic with what you can achieve, don't overwhelm yourself. Focus on what you do best and outsource the rest!

Learn, research, and track your symptoms.

Learning from the experts, Dr Louise Newson, on Instagram is great.

Research menopause in your spare time and get an understanding of what the hell is going on in your body.

Track your symptoms so you can identify the main triggers for you and reduce your ASSS! (Triple S!) Alcohol, Sugar, Spice & Stress!

Try and focus on the positives, like not having a monthly cycle to deal with anymore!

Remember, you have a choice in 90% of situations, so it's up to you to make the right choices for you and how you're feeling.

Track your energy levels:

If you're struggling with fatigue and your energy levels, start tracking your energy with the moon cycles as an experiment. It has been a real game-changer for me. It doesn't need to be in-depth, and you don't need to be an expert.

Mental agility exercises

Mental agility is important to keep those brain cells working, and it also helps with forgetfulness. I try to do mental arithmetic a bit more even though maths isn't my strong point, so I think I'm going to learn a language instead! You could try board games, sudoku, or anything that taxes your brain a little!

Most of all, do what feels good for you and find your support network.

Her Memorable Moment: I could just about disguise being overwhelmingly hot, but the sweat would make my make-up run, and my mascara would start sliding down my face.

How did/does menopause affect you in your working life?

The main symptom for me was extreme hot flushes. Most of my clients work in the construction industry. I was travelling up and down to London from the Midlands three or four times a week, running workshops, attending high-level meetings, and interacting with a mainly male workforce. In a second, I could go from normal to bright red and literally dripping with sweat. Bizarrely my glasses would fall off my nose – I never knew the sides of my nose could sweat so much! The travelling was hell. The train journey down to London and back would inevitably mean being squashed in next to someone and getting hotter and hotter until, on occasions, I thought I might pass out. The tube was a nightmare. Wherever I was, I used to find myself constantly tipping my head forward and trying to blow air over my chest to cool down – not a good look.

What was/is the biggest challenge for you?

The biggest challenge was to try and pretend nothing was happening. Trying to keep the hot flushes in check with frequent trips to the loo was tricky.

I found the whole thing embarrassing and worried that clients would see me as a menopausal (i.e. old) woman rather than someone with great experience who could really add value to their business. Then it started to chip away at my confidence until, quite honestly, I started to see myself as a menopausal (i.e. old) woman rather than the dynamic, energetic person I'd always been.

I also had to select my clothing carefully – aiming for loose styles and natural fabrics - and aligning that with my professional style was a challenge as I am a tall and curvy woman.

What worked/works for you to manage/cope?

HRT. I was concerned about starting HRT and didn't really want to go down that road. But something had to change. Luckily, my GP is an expert in women's health and really took time to go through everything with me – all the pros and cons. She was with me every step of the way as I tried different methods and doses until we hit upon the right way for me. I've never looked back. The flushes stopped within a couple of weeks, and I was back to normal – but better.

I have more energy and zest for life, my hair is thicker and stronger, and my skin is great – glowing. If I have more than a couple of glasses of red wine at the weekend, I can get the odd hot flush at night, but nothing compared to before. For me, the benefits outweigh the small risks, and I'm comfortable that I've chosen the best way forward for me.

I also take daily vitamin supplements, eat a balanced diet, and get plenty of fresh air and exercise. I meditate and can honestly say that I have more confidence now than I have for a long time.

If you could share one piece of advice for women going through the same, what would it be?

Find a doctor who specialises in women's health and talk to them about what you can do and what's best for you. If you decide to take HRT, don't just rely on that – take a holistic approach and look at your diet, what you do in your spare time, your sleep patterns, your relaxation methods, and throw everything at it.

Dawn's Story

Her Memorable Moment: Standing stark naked on the balcony (well, it was a hot summer in France), shouting at my beloved in the garden below all because he asked me yet again *for some help in the garden.* I was at breaking point with too many things to attend to as a solopreneur, so in a crazy fit of temper, I threw my laptop over the balcony to get his attention and shouted, 'yes, of course I'll stop working, what would you like me to do'? It was a wake-up call for both of us.

How did menopause affect you in your working life?

I'm post-menopausal. It was a few years ago now, and my periods had been light for decades, so I had to think hard about this because I was in denial about it for a long time. I asked my husband if he remembered anything about that time and he said I was my usual 'even tempered self' which was kind of him considering the laptop incident.

As much as I suffered during the night, my days were fairly symptom-free, other than being ridiculously tired at work. I was sleep deprived due to infuriating bouts of insomnia and terrible night sweats which had me drenched, so I was frequently showering and changing my nightdress, which made me finally admit menopause was a real thing. In fact, I suffered for two long years.

Now I'm annoyed with myself about how in my usual superwomen style, I struggled through it – alone - not realising there were alternatives to HRT or even professionals I could have talked to. Towards the end, I discovered Borage Oil, and that drastically and quickly improved my night symptoms. As a holistic practitioner, I really should have been more aware and practiced better self-care.

I suspect if I'd still been working in a corporate environment where I'd been suited and booted, and made up, wanting to appear cool and business-like, then anxiety about having hot flushes could have been worse.

I used to joke about looking forward to menopause, saying *it'll be the first time I feel warm* because vegetarians tend to have thinner blood, so I'm always cold, but the reality is it's no joke!

What was the biggest challenge for you?

Despite being somebody who said *I'm not going to be one of those women who blame weight gain on the M word*, it happened. The bloating and weight gain has been hard as I've always been weight-obsessed, and body conscious and I really feel it's out of my control now, which is frustrating. Gut health is so important, and being brought up vegetarian, I knew I had a good grounding, but I was probably too blasé about it. My mum laughed at how I didn't believe her when she talked about how much your body changes - every decade. I really thought it was a case of mind over matter. Whilst having a positive mental attitude does indeed help, you cannot control your hormones. You need help from experts with supporting supplements.

Then there's the lack of libido. It disappeared overnight. It was like a light switch going off. After having a healthy sexual appetite, I was highly embarrassed at having to admit to my beloved, 'it's not you, it's me - I've stopped thinking about sex, and I just don't feel anything'. That was absolutely the worst symptom for me. Consequently, it's something I really worked hard to fix, more so than any other symptom. Thank goodness for a thoughtful and patient partner who didn't give up on me.

If you could share one piece of advice, what would it be?

Don't struggle alone, and don't be embarrassed to get help for whatever symptom is troubling you, even a personal subject like your sex life, and make sure you talk to your partner about what you're going through because they're not mind-readers.

If you know your diet isn't the best, find a better one, and take up an exercise you enjoy; movement of any kind is so important, and remember your self-care and beauty regime can have a profound effect on your sense of well-being too.

Don't accept the situation if you're not happy. However, once you've done everything you possibly can to help yourself, learn to accept the positives and look for new opportunities in the next chapter of your life.

Angie's Story

Her Memorable Moment: The feeling of walking into my new head gardener role for a childhood dream garden. Knowing I've got this and even though the journey was hard. It was worth every second.

How did menopause affect you in your working life?

In my working life, menopause affected me a lot, because I went into surgical menopause when I was 44. I had a hysterectomy, and I had no idea what was coming on the day of the operation. I was told on the day that basically that they were going to take my ovaries. So literally the next day, I went straight into menopause. I was a gardener before the operation, and I knew that I wouldn't be able to go straight back into gardening because my core wouldn't be working. So, for me, I went from what I call normal to being like a nanny, literally overnight. I couldn't think. I couldn't concentrate. I had bad emotional outbursts. I was having hot flushes, I had every single menopausal symptom going. I was such an organised person, but I literally couldn't think, I couldn't concentrate, I couldn't get any clarity, which then puts you right into this downward spiral. Because then you start to think if I can't concentrate, I can't think, I can't do my job, I can't work. And you kind of go into a massive spiral, really.

So, I guess menopause at the initial stages for me was really debilitating. I couldn't work at all. I think that just through reading and learning, I then started to do things I should be doing. And I then realised that through exercise classes, I could get my core back. I had to go work in an office temporarily last January, and it was awful. I worked in an office before gardening. I felt like I couldn't do my job. And that was menopause. I know that now. Because now that I think I'm through most of it and with HRT, and back to gardening, I can concentrate, I can forward plan. My brain isn't doing all these hundreds of things at once.

What was/is the biggest challenge for you?

I don't know if I'm definitely through menopause, because obviously being on HRT alleviates all the symptoms. But even if I'm in the middle of it. All I would say is that you must find what works for you really, it's such an individual journey. I guess I was, in a way, lucky that I was put directly into it. I didn't have the lead up to it. But when I look back, I think perimenopause, in my mid-'30s, but I just didn't have constant hot flushes. I just had them every now and again. I think, in a way I've been quite lucky in that extent, I guess, in that it was sort of everything at once.

I have never ever in my life suffered from anxiety and confidence issues. I just felt extremely anxious. I had no confidence, no self-esteem, really. It just completely bottomed out; I had nothing. And I was getting rejections from jobs that I applied for. And people were telling me I was overqualified. And I've never experienced that in my whole life. I've always had a job. And I think for me, that was the biggest thing, the things like the hot flushes, and then no sleeping. Once I knew what you could do to help those, I learned how to deal with them. But the lack of self-confidence and anxiety was hard for me. And I think the older you get, which is mostly when this appears, unfortunately, the harder it is. And I think it's those two elements, the anxiety and confidence issues, that I found the hardest.

What worked/works for you to manage/cope?

Yeah, so it is a massive array of things that helped me. I paid privately to speak to Diane Danzebrink in the end. It wasn't a lot, but it was beneficial. And she explained to me basically that I had no oestrogen at all and that the amount they were giving me was so minimal, and to bring me to a level, I needed to take a higher dose of HRT. The other thing was reading lots of books. I had all this time, especially when I was healing from the operation. I realised then that I had to completely change how I was eating. When you get to this age, you need so many units, so much calcium, so much vitamin D. I now take magnesium and zinc just before I go to bed because that's what helps you sleep. If you take magnesium one tablet before you go to bed, it knocks you out.

And things like looking after your gut is so important. It affects your brain; it affects levels in your brain, so good gut health. So, things like kefir, sauerkraut, which I cannot stand and kimchi, things like that, that put good bugs back into your gut. They had a massive effect on things like anxiety, brain health, confidence. And then I think just moving more, because honestly, I was quite a slender girl, before my operation, I then had the operation. And I became a nanny overnight. All my muscle turned to what I call nanny legs, what I used to see on my nan. You don't have any muscle definition, and it happened almost overnight. I've been told that is quite common. So, you've got to keep moving. You must do high-intensity workouts because you've got to improve things like bone strength and really start looking after yourself. So, I would say it's a mixture of two things, it's your diet, and the right supplements. It's HRT, or if you don't want to, or can't take HRT, then an equivalent, and it's altering your diet with things that help you, i.e., lots of seeds. Then adding in lots and lots of exercise, but short spats of high intensity, so like 10-20 minutes a day maximum and it's done. Just keep moving.

So, it is a mixture of lots and lots of things. And I think also being really kind to yourself. So don't worry about the little things. So many times, I worried about little things. And yeah, you might have days where you just think to yourself, oh my god, what's going on? And you do develop this thing where you have no filter. But sometimes, it's not a bad thing. Get it out there, sometimes! It isn't a bad thing; you do develop that. I think menopause is a learning curve of lots of little things. And I think if you can pick off one bit of time, a bit like in a piece of cake, take a piece of that cake each time and deal with it. And then move to the next piece of cake. And if you can't move to the next one, don't worry about it. But just do a little bit at a time because otherwise, the cake looks huge.

If you could share one piece of advice, what would it be?

Top tip: Read around. Don't be afraid to reach out to people. I reached out to somebody who's quite high profile on menopause on Instagram. She did a consultation over the phone with me. And yes, I had to pay £80 for an hour, but she wrote to my GP, and she got me my HRT. She gave me the information in a nice report, which gave the doctor all the information she needed to prescribe my medication. I think the most important thing I can say to somebody is to join a local group. Look at everything, Instagram, find anything you can read. Listen to podcasts. Just get as much information as you can so that you can make sensible decisions about what is right for you.

I must admit that HRT is the only thing that stopped the hot flushes for me. But I know other things work for other people.

The only other thing I would say really get some help through reading and listening to Liz Earle and Diane Danzebrink podcasts.

How does menopause affect you in your working life?

For a bit of background - I work in a secondary school, the pastoral department, and I'm also in the process of setting up my own coaching business.

Well, I've gone through a bit of a transition with managing menopause. Before I would say that I would wake up feeling tired. I didn't know what day it was or what I had in my diary. Being a focused and organised person, these changes made me feel totally out of my depth, and at one point, I didn't even know if I could do my job properly. I was in a bit of a mess.

There were days when I felt like I'd been hit with a sledge-hammer. I was just not me. I then had a bit of a wake-up call, and kind of took myself to task as in reminding myself menopause is normal. This happens to every single woman that has come before me and will come after me. I told myself, 'you've just got to get on with it, girl'.

What was/is the biggest challenge for you?

I looked at my diet, and I looked at the way I exercise because I believed I was healthy. I felt that I exercised well, but my body was telling me it wasn't happy. I always looked upon menopause as something I wasn't going to go through because it just sounded horrendous. When I was younger, I would say that menopause was not for me, and if I had to go through it, it would be for just one day, I would be 72 and on the 24th June. Now I know it was just tongue in cheek, but there was an element of belief that I couldn't possibly go through something which could potentially rob me of me and who I was/am.

What worked/works for you to manage/cope?

I realised that, instead of fighting my body, I must look after it. If this were a child or a loved one, we would look after them. We would nurture and cherish them to carry them through it. So, I learned how to talk properly to myself and my body. I looked at everything that I ate, and I realised that a lot of the foods I ate was not actually good for me. There were an awful lot of chemicals. So now, I've gone completely over to just eating natural products, cooking from scratch, not that I was a microwave dinner person before. I just wanted to eat more healthily. I looked at my exercise routine as well. Instead of running three miles on the treadmill, to which my body was saying, "No, please don't do that", I do more resistance stuff now.

But the main thing for me was to comfort my body through this transition. I talk to it. So, if my skin looks like a crocodile that died three years ago, I'd say to my body, 'Oh, you're looking a bit dry. Come on, let's find you some moisturiser.'

Then I developed a health mantra. And my mantra is:

"I take care of my body, my mind, and my soul because that is where I live, and I live where I am nourished, nurtured, cherished and loved."

And so, this is how I am approaching menopause, I'm actually nurturing my body through it. And I wish that I had done that when I went through adolescence. Because we're so angry at adolescence, aren't we?

I think my main symptom now is that there are moments when I feel like I've put the central heating on. It really is a rather settling symptom.

I used to suffer a lot from fluid retention, and by adopting this new approach, I don't get it as much now. I drink lots of water now, which is another nourishing thing to do for your body, especially when you're going through all this.

I think the message out there is that menopause is horrendous, and it's awful, and we can become so negative towards our body that we don't actually nurture it and comfort it through this transition, which I think is what we/l need to do.

Another thing is I always try and do is work out what triggers my hot flushes. I've found that it's when I'm feeling a bit challenged or slightly anxious. So, then the more I've dealt with that, the less hot flushes I have.

I think my biggest challenge is the state of my face. It looks old half the time. But I am learning that this is more about my perception. And that's what I've got to overcome. I've always had a very young-looking face. And since I was 50, which is now four years ago, it has aged considerably, and I don't like that because it is such a change to what I have been used to. It's the whole concept of ageing and losing your youthfulness. When it's your face, it becomes more of a focus because you can hide everything else.

The reality is we need to accept our whole body and look after it. I have facials, and I do look after my skin, so I'm doing the right things. The girl looking back at you in the mirror is still the girl. You know, despite the wrinkles and the slight sagging skin, she's still there. You need to love yourself through this; it really is the only way.

I'm very mindful of my mantra that I live inside my body, and I want to feel looked after. I want to feel cherished and loved, so I'm going to love my body. And some days, that's harder than others. But I think if that is in the forefront of your mind, every day, you will come through this because it's a journey you're going through together, you and your body.

And where I work in a school, I find that I'm one of the oldest ones there now. Teachers look like they are twelve, but I am beginning to find that I'm happy now to say, yes, I'm in my '50s. Whereas before, I felt like I was competing, and not very well, if I am honest. But now I'm quite happy in my own skin.

With the acceptance of menopause, you are actually accepting yourself as well.

Sometimes you wish you could start all over again with the knowledge and wisdom you've got now. Regardless of menopause, we need to look after ourselves.

If you could share one piece of advice, what would it be?

Top Tip: Be kind to yourself and cherish your body. Love your body through this because it's a journey you're going through together. You're not fighting with one another. Love your body through it. Comfort your body, and comfort it healthily.

11

_____

FINAL WORDS

This brings us to the end of our fabulous journey through menopause. We hope we have inspired you, encouraged you, and made you smile as you have read the book.

We are two friends with a *burning* (*haha*) desire to help women power through their menopause, learn tips and tricks, and see the funny side of what can feel like a monumental time in your life.

We hope you feel less alone and have learned strategies from us and our brave ladies that you can adapt to your circumstances, as you run your small business or work in a corporate setting.

We would absolutely love to hear from you on what you enjoyed the most about the book, so feel free to send an email to either of us. You will find our contact details on the next page.

We would like to leave you with one final tip: If you are having a hot flush, open your freezer door and take in the cool, chilled air. It works a treat! (*The experience can be even better with a chilled Prosecco in your hand!*)

12

REFLECTIVE WORKBOOK

You will have noticed throughout the book that we mention our Reflective Workbook.

We don't like writing responses in our books, so thought you might not enjoy that either, so we have created a lovely Reflective Workbook that contains all of the questions we've asked you in one place.

Get your Reflective Workbook, and while you're there, check out our podcast show, Mind Over Menopause.

WHAT'S NEXT?

Contact Gail:

Email: gail@gailmgibson.com

Phone:

+60 147 730769

(Malaysia office)

+44 7950 193312

(UK office)

Website www.gailmgibson.com

LinkedIn

https://www.linkedin.com/in/gailmgibson/

The Can Do Way Podcast

https://audiowallah.com/category/the-can-do-way/

Women Leaders Network

https://www.linkedin.com/groups/10547330/

Personalised Coaching and Mentoring:

- 1:1 and Team Peak Personal Performance Coaching for Business & Corporate
- Becoming Agile to Thrive
- The COVID Painkiller
- The Coach in YOU
- Women Leaders Self-Leadership Mastermind Programme
- Corporate Coaching and Mentorship Program for SEE-19© Leaders.

Contact Ruby:

Email: ruby@rubymcguire.com

Phone: +44 7920 260111

(UK office)

Website: www.rubymcguire.com

LinkedIn: https://www.linkedin.com/in/rubymcguirecoaching/

Rock Your Fabulous Biz Podcast

https://podcasts.apple.com/gb/podcast/rock-your-fabulous-biz-podcast/id992518319

Personalised Coaching and Mentoring:

- 1:1 Coaching & Mentoring to become Queen of your business, work savvy, up level your mindset and biz

- Queen of Business Mastermind
- Fearless Visibility Diva Programme
- Discovery Call Magic Programme
- Cappuccino Coaching Club
- Rock Your Visibility

Milton Keynes UK
Ingram Content Group UK Ltd.
UKHW020610130923
428584UK00012B/314